How to Use This Book

Look for these special features in this book:

SIDEBARS, **CHARTS**, **GRAPHS**, and original **MAPS** expand your understanding of what's being discussed—and also make useful sources for classroom reports.

FAQs answer common **F**requently **A**sked **Q**uestions about people, places, and things.

WOW FACTORS offer "Who knew?" facts to keep you thinking.

TRAVEL GUIDE gives you tips on exploring the state—either in person or right from your chair!

PROJECT ROOM provides fun ideas for school assignments and incredible research projects. Plus, there's a guide to primary sources—what they are and how to cite them.

Please note: All statistics are as up-to-date as possible at the time of publication. Population data is taken from the 2010 census.

Consultants: Marvin P. Carlson, Professor and Research Geologist, University of Nebraska; William Loren Katz; Susan Wunder, Associate Professor, University of Nebraska–Lincoln; Dan Holtz, Professor, Peru State College

Book production by The Design Lab

Library of Congress Cataloging-in-Publication Data
Heinrichs, Ann.
 Nebraska / by Ann Heinrichs. — Revised edition.
  pages cm. — (America, the beautiful. Third series)
 Includes bibliographical references and index.
 ISBN 978-0-531-24892-8 (lib. bdg.)
 1. Nebraska—Juvenile literature. I. Title.
 F666.3.H454 2014
 978.2—dc23   2013032479

1 2 3 4 5 6 7 8 9 10 R 23 22 21 20 19 18 17 16 15 14

Nebraska

BY ANN HEINRICHS

Third Series, Revised Edition

Children's Press®
An Imprint of Scholastic Inc.
New York ★ Toronto ★ London ★ Auckland ★ Sydney
Mexico City ★ New Delhi ★ Hong Kong
Danbury, Connecticut

CONTENTS

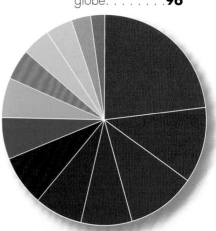

Witness the mass migration of pioneers across Nebraska's plains. See how the Homestead Act, telegraph lines, and railroads changed Nebraskans' lives. . . **44**

GROWTH AND CHANGE

4

MORE MODERN TIMES

5

Depression and drought hurt the state, but Nebraskans took control and rose up strong. . . **60**

9 TRAVEL GUIDE

Stroll through a pioneer village, plant a tree, explore the Badlands, and whoop it up at a Wild West show. That's just a smattering of all you can see and do in Nebraska. **104**

PROJECT ROOM

★

★

MINNESOTA

SOUTH DAKOTA

WYOMING

Toadstool Park

Badlands

Niobrara

Nebraska
National
Forest

Lewis and Clark
Campsite

Missouri

IOWA

NIOBRARA

Sandhills → Sand Hills

SCOTTSBLUFF

Chimney
Rock

North Platte

Oregon
Trail

NEBRASKA

College Baseball
World Series

Nebraska
State Capitol

OMAHA

Missouri

Panorama
Point

South Platte

Lake McConaughy

Great Platte River Road
Archway Monument

KEARNEY

Harold Warp
Pioneer Village

Republican

Loup

Platte

GRAND ISLAND

LINCOLN

Henry
Doorly
Zoo

Platte River

BEATRICE

Homestead Natio
Monument of Ame

COLORADO

0   50
Miles

KANSAS

QUICK FACTS

State capital: Lincoln
Largest city: Omaha
Total area: 77,354 square miles
(200,347 sq km)
Highest point: Panorama Point, 5,424
feet (1,653 m), located in Kimball
County
Lowest point: Missouri River at 840
feet (256 m) in Richardson County

Welcome to Nebraska!

HOW DID NEBRASKA GET ITS NAME?

The story of Nebraska's name begins with a river. The Platte River is the major river running across Nebraska. Native Oto people called it *Nebrathka,* meaning "flat water." In 1714, French explorer Étienne de Véniard, Sieur de Bourgmont, reached the mouth of the Platte. Hearing the Oto word, he called the river *Nebraskier.* Later, explorer John C. Frémont called it the Nebraska River. Meanwhile, French fur trappers called it the *Rivière de Plat* or *Rivière Platte,* French for "flat river." In the 1840s, Congress began thinking of creating a new U.S. territory in that region. But what should it be called? William Wilkins, the U.S. secretary of war, had an idea: "The Platte or Nebraska River being the central stream would very properly furnish a name to the territory." The name Nebraska was chosen, and it stuck!

8

READ ABOUT

Chimney Rock, in
western Nebraska

CHAPTER ONE

LAND

★

NEBRASKA IS PART OF THE NATION'S GREAT PLAINS REGION—A VAST EXPANSE OF GRASSLANDS AND TREELESS PLAINS. But it is no arid wasteland. It covers 77,354 square miles (200,347 square kilometers), and about 93 percent of that is ranch or farmland. This land is not flat but a series of rolling plains that peak in the far west, at Panorama Point. At 5,424 feet (1,653 meters), it's Nebraska's highest point. The state's lowest point is in the southeastern corner, by the Missouri River, at 840 feet (256 m) above sea level. In between these extremes, leafy green corn and golden wheat stretch as far as the eye can see.

Q8 WHY ISN'T THE MIDWEST JUST CALLED THE MIDDLE?

A8 In the early days of the United States, the country was very narrow, east to west. The Appalachian Mountains were seen as the westernmost part of the country. As explorers pushed farther west, people realized that much more land lay west of the Appalachians than they had thought. The nearer western lands came to be called the Middle West, or Midwest, and lands near the Pacific coast came to be called the Far West, or just the West.

LAND REGIONS

On a map of the United States, Nebraska looks like it's almost in the center of the country. The U.S. Census Bureau calls Nebraska one of the Midwest states. From a geographic point of view, Nebraska is also a Great Plains state. In area, it is the 16th-largest state. It's bordered by South Dakota on the north and Kansas to the south. Iowa and Missouri lie to the east, and Colorado and Wyoming are to the west. Nebraska has two major land regions—the Dissected Till Plains region and the Great Plains region.

The Dissected Till Plains

Hundreds of thousands of years ago, gigantic glaciers scoured the land. They carved out a landscape of gently rolling hills in the eastern one-fifth of Nebraska. As the

Nebraska Geo-Facts

Along with the state's geographical highlights, this chart ranks Nebraska's land, water, and total area compared to all other states.

Total area; rank . . . . . . 77,354 square miles (200,347 sq km); 16th
Land; rank . . . . 76,872 square miles (199,098 sq km); 15th
Water; rank . . . . 481 square miles (1,246 sq km); 42nd
Inland water; rank . . . . 481 square miles (1,246 sq km); 34th
Geographic center . . . . Custer County,
Latitude . . . . 40° N to 43° N
Longitude . . . . 95° 25' W to 104° W
Highest point . . . . Panorama Point, 5,424 feet (1,653 m),
located in Kimball County
Lowest point . . . . Missouri River at 840 feet (256 m) in Richardson County
Largest city . . . . Omaha
Longest river . . . . Missouri River, 385 miles (620 km)

Source: U.S. Census Bureau, 2010 census

Nebraska is slightly larger than South Dakota and slightly smaller than Kansas. Rhode Island could fit inside Nebraska almost 50 times!

Nebraska's Platte River flows through the state's green prairies.

glaciers melted, they left behind deposits of rich soil, forming material called till. Blowing winds then deposited dusty soil called loess on top of the till. Rivers and streams dissect, or cut through, this land, creating deep river valleys. So geologists call the area the Dissected Till Plains region.

Thanks to its fertile soil, eastern Nebraska grows abundant crops. Crops grow so well in this region that it's called the nation's breadbasket. Corn is Nebraska's major crop, and it's mostly grown here on the eastern plains. It's part of a region in the country's Midwest called the Corn Belt. Nebraska's largest cities—Omaha and Lincoln, the state capital—grew up in this fertile region.

Nebraska Topography

Use the color-coded elevation chart to see on the map Nebraska's high points (dark red to orange) and low points (green to dark green). Elevation is measured as the distance above or below sea level.

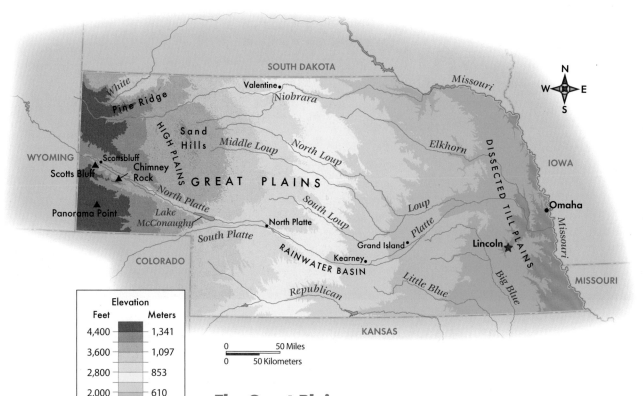

Elevation	
Feet	**Meters**
4,400	1,341
3,600	1,097
2,800	853
2,000	610
1,200	366

0   50 Miles
0   50 Kilometers

The Great Plains

The rest of Nebraska lies within the Great Plains. Nebraska's Great Plains region is divided into several sections, each with special features.

The area north of the Platte River in central Nebraska is called the Sand Hills region. Its name is a perfect description. Wind has blown the sandy soil into hills, or sand dunes. If you flew over the Sand Hills, you'd see that it has a bumpy, wavy surface. This is the largest area of sand dunes in North America.

Cattle graze the natural prairie of Nebraska's Sand Hills.

Crops don't grow well in the Sand Hills. It's said that most of this region has never been touched by a plow. However, tall grasses grow on the hills. They keep the soil in place so it won't erode. Many Nebraska ranchers graze their cattle in the Sand Hills, taking care not to overgraze the land.

South-central Nebraska, just south of the Platte River, is sometimes called the Rainwater Basin. It's a moist region, with many wetlands and small lakes. Millions of **migrating** birds roost there in the spring and fall. Much of southern Nebraska is covered by a deep layer of the wind-borne loess. As heat and water break down the loess over time, minerals that aid plant growth are released. This type of soil makes for highly productive farmland.

WORD TO KNOW

migrating *traveling to another location, usually covering a long distance*

Toadstool Park, located within Nebraska's Oglala National Grasslands, is filled with hundreds of unusual toadstool rock formations.

WORD TO KNOW

buttes *narrow, flat-topped hills with very steep sides*

Western Nebraska is called the Panhandle. It looks like a handle sticking out from the rest of the state, which is the pan. Most of the Panhandle is in the High Plains region. The High Plains are dry, with short grasses and tough little bushes. Here and there, **buttes** and other rock formations tower above the plains. A butte called Chimney Rock rises in western Nebraska. For westbound pioneers in the 1800s, it was a well-known landmark. Panorama Point is Nebraska's highest point. It rises in the far southwest corner of the Panhandle. Panorama Point is neither a mountain nor a hill. It's just a little rise in the landscape of the plains.

One section of Nebraska's High Plains region is called the Pine Ridge. It's in the northwest, between the White and Niobrara rivers. The Pine Ridge is known for its high cliffs, deep canyons, and pine forests. Nebraska's far northwest corner is called the Badlands. Here, wind and water have worn the sandstone rocks into weirdly beautiful shapes. One area is called Toadstool Park. Its rock formations look like—you guessed it!—toadstools.

RIVERS, LAKES, AND AQUIFERS

Rivers were Nebraska's earliest "highways." Native Americans, explorers, and settlers traveled on them. The Missouri River runs along Nebraska's eastern and northeastern borders. It forms the dividing line between Nebraska and Missouri, Iowa, and part of South Dakota. The Missouri is the major tributary of the Mississippi River, the country's largest river. Omaha, Nebraska's biggest city, lies on the west bank of the Missouri.

Within Nebraska, the Platte River is the major waterway. It begins in western Nebraska, where the North Platte and South Platte rivers come together near the city of North Platte. From there, it runs eastward across the state. Finally, the Platte empties into the Missouri River near Omaha. In the 1800s, thousands of westbound pioneers rode their wagons alongside the Platte River. Grand Island, Kearney, and North Platte grew up as supply centers along the route.

The major rivers in northern Nebraska are the Niobrara, Elkhorn, and Loup rivers. The Niobrara River, in the far north, flows into the Missouri River. It's one of the most popular canoeing rivers in the country. The Elkhorn and Loup rivers run through the Sand Hills and empty into the Platte River. The Republican, Big Blue, and Little Blue rivers flow through southern Nebraska. All three eventually empty into the Kansas River in Kansas.

Hundreds of small lakes are scattered throughout Nebraska. Many are in the Sand Hills region. Nebraska's largest lake is Lake McConaughy. It's a reservoir, or artifi-

SEE IT HERE!

TOADSTOOL PARK

Toadstool Park is a wonderland of strange rock formations. Horizontal stripes across the rocks show layers of material deposited over millions of years. The park also contains the **fossil** remains of ancient animals. Camels, pigs, rhinoceroses, turtles, and creatures called beardogs left their skeletons behind. The camel family originated in North America millions of years ago, and some types of rhino may have originated here, too. Visitors may not remove any fossils from the park. Scientists are studying the fossils to piece together Nebraska's ancient history.

WORD TO KNOW

fossil *the remains or prints of ancient animals or plants left in stone*

Nebraska's Lake McConaughy Recreation Area is a popular summertime destination.

WORD TO KNOW

aquifer *an underground layer of soil or loose rock that holds water*

cial lake created to store water. It was formed by Kingsley Dam on the North Platte River. Lake McConaughy and many other reservoirs were created to provide irrigation water for farms. About one-fourth of Nebraska's farmland is irrigated. However, most of the state's irrigation water comes from underground sources.

Nebraska sits on top of the Ogallala (High Plains) **Aquifer**. The aquifer is hundreds of feet deep. It consists of sand, gravel, and silt eroded from the Rocky Mountains and now saturated with rich deposits of groundwater. Stretching from South Dakota to Texas, these saturated deposits are among the largest groundwater reservoirs in the world. Nebraskans have dug tens of thousands of wells to pump water from the aquifer onto the cropland. Sprinkler systems irrigate circular fields that are easily visible both from airplanes and in satellite imagery.

CLIMATE

Nebraskans like to say that if you don't like the weather, wait five minutes—it will change. Nebraskans live through sweltering heat and bitter cold. Average temperatures are not all that extreme. The average temperature in July is about 76 degrees Fahrenheit (24 degrees Celsius), and January averages about 23°F (–5°C). But sudden changes in weather, and extreme hot and cold spells, are common. A stretch of summer days can be well over 100°F (38°C), and a winter cold snap can plunge way below 0°F (–18°C).

Northeastern Nebraska gets the coldest winters. The west and southwest are not quite as cold. In the summer, southeastern Nebraska gets the hottest weather. But in the Panhandle, summertime temperatures are rather mild.

Most of Nebraska's rain falls from April through September. That's great for crops during their growing season. Some years, though, farmers are plagued with **drought**. Eastern Nebraska gets the most rain and snow, while the west is much drier. The heaviest snows fall in late winter.

WORD TO KNOW

drought *a period of little or no rainfall*

Weather Report

TEMPERATURE **118°F**

TEMPERATURE **-47°F**

This chart shows record temperatures (high and low) for the state, as well as average temperatures (July and January) and average annual precipitation.

Record high temperature . . . . 118°F (48°C) at Minden on July 24, 1936; at Hartington on July 17, 1936; and at Geneva on July 15, 1934

Record low temperature –47°F (–44°C) at Bridgeport, on February 12, 1899; and at Oshkosh on December 22, 1989

Average January temperature . . . . .23°F (–5°C)
Average July temperature . . . . 76°F (24°C)
Average yearly precipitation . . . . 23 inches (58 cm)

Source: National Climatic Data Center, NESDIS, NOAA, U.S. Department of Commerce

18

Tornadoes are a common sight in Nebraska during summertime.

Run for Cover!

Nebraskans say they have more than their share of wicked weather. They suffer through blizzards, thunderstorms, windstorms, hailstorms, dust storms, and tornadoes.

People run for cover when the golf-ball–sized hailstones come crashing down. Nebraska gets more hailstorms than almost anywhere else in the country. Heavy thunderstorms break out in the spring and summer. Sometimes they're so heavy that the rivers overflow their banks, flooding farms and towns. Tornadoes whip through Nebraska, too. In dry years, dust storms swirl across the Panhandle. The dust clouds can be so thick that drivers cannot see the car ahead of them.

Blizzards, or fierce snowstorms, often sweep across the plains. Blizzards in the winter of 1948 to 1949 dumped more than 100 inches (250 centimeters) of snow on parts of Nebraska. People trapped in their farmhouses had to burn furniture to keep warm. In one area, the snowdrifts were 30 feet (9 m) high and didn't melt until June!

ANIMAL LIFE

Bird-watchers from around the world come to see Nebraska's sandhill cranes. Half a million of these long-legged birds descend on the state every spring. They settle on a stretch of the Platte River between Grand Island and Kearney. They can be seen feeding in the cornfields and roosting by the river.

Huge herds of bison, or buffalo, once grazed across Nebraska's grassy plains. But by the 1800s, hunters had wiped out almost all of these magnificent animals. Today, only a few protected herds survive in the state.

Deer, antelope, and elk are some of Nebraska's larger wild animals. The state's largest herd of bighorn sheep, a type of mountain sheep, lives in the rough, rocky Pine Ridge region. Smaller animals include coyotes,

Sandhill cranes wading near Nebraska's Platte River

SHALL WE DANCE?

Sandhill cranes begin swooping into Nebraska in March—and they just keep coming. Numbering about 500,000, they create the largest gathering of sandhill cranes in the world. They stop on their migration from their winter homes in Mexico, Texas, and New Mexico. When they leave, they continue on to Canada, Alaska, and even Siberia, in northern Russia.

At sunrise and sunset, the cranes roost along the Platte River. During the day, they feast in the nearby cornfields. The corn gives them energy for their long flight ahead. For many crane watchers, the most exciting spectacle is the cranes' "dance." Pairs of cranes engage in an elaborate mating display—bowing, stretching out their wings, and leaping into the air. Cranes mate for life. Their dance is a way of establishing a partnership or strengthening their bond.

ENDANGERED SPECIES

Almost 30 animal and plant species in Nebraska are becoming scarce. Some are listed as endangered, meaning they are nearly **extinct**. Others are listed as threatened, meaning they may soon become endangered. Two of the birds that are disappearing are the piping plover and the interior least tern. Both live along the sandy banks of rivers and streams. Black-footed ferrets are disappearing from the plains. Many other birds, mammals, fish, insects, and plants are threatened or endangered. For some, their natural habitat is disappearing; others may be victims of pesticides. Nebraska has passed a number of laws to protect and preserve its fragile wildlife.

A black-footed ferret

beavers, prairie dogs, raccoons, muskrats, rabbits, pheasants, quail, squirrels, and wild turkeys. Mountain lions had disappeared from the state by about 1900. But they began wandering back into western Nebraska in the 1990s. Nebraska's wildlife officials are eager to protect them so they can thrive in the state once again.

WORD TO KNOW

extinct *no longer existing*

Nebraska National Park Areas

This map shows some of Nebraska's national parks, monuments, preserves, and other areas protected by the National Park Service.

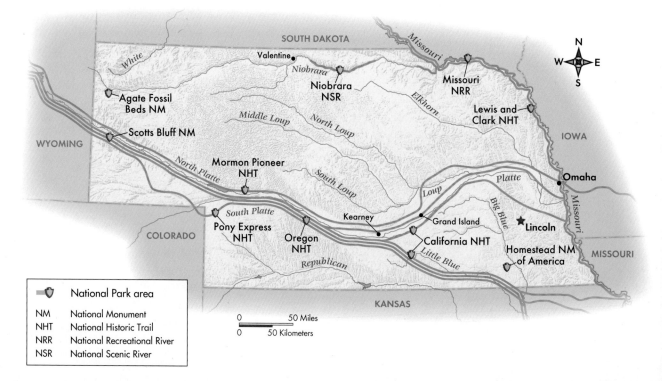

NM	National Monument
NHT	National Historic Trail
NRR	National Recreational River
NSR	National Scenic River

National Park area

0   50 Miles
0   50 Kilometers

PLANT LIFE

Only about 3 percent of Nebraska is forestland. But Nebraska is big on planting trees. In fact, from 1895 until 1945, Nebraska's official nickname was the Tree Planters' State. The world's largest hand-planted forest is the Nebraska National Forest near Halsey. People planted more than a million cedar and pine trees there in the early 1900s.

Arbor Day began in Nebraska, too. It's a national holiday devoted to tree planting. J. Sterling Morton of Nebraska City established the holiday in 1872. At first, it was just a local holiday. But in time, tree-planting

MINI-BIO

J. STERLING MORTON: TREE LOVER

J. Sterling Morton (1832–1902) loved trees. Born in New York, he moved to Nebraska City in 1854. A dedicated conservationist, Morton encouraged people to plant trees on Nebraska's plains. The trees would prevent soil erosion by acting as windbreaks and holding the soil in place. They would also provide shade from the sun and beautify the landscape. Morton founded Arbor Day in 1872. He also served as secretary of agriculture under President Grover Cleveland.

? **Want to know more?** Visit www.factsfornow.scholastic.com and enter the keyword **Nebraska**.

Little of Nebraska is covered with trees. The Nebraska National Forest is an exception.

A bison walks across the Nebraska prairie.

fever spread around the country. Today, the United States celebrates Arbor Day on the last Friday in April. Nebraska City is the headquarters of the National Arbor Day Foundation.

Grasslands cover much of the state. They are great for grazing cattle. Bluestem, grama, and buffalo grass are the most common grass species. Nebraska's Sand Hills region has the largest area of sandhill grasslands in the Western Hemisphere. In Nebraska's northwest corner is the Oglala National Grassland. Covering almost 95,000 acres (38,000 hectares), it's like a great sea of prairie grasses.

PROTECTING THE ENVIRONMENT

Because farming is so important to the state, Nebraskans work hard to preserve their soil and water. Soil erosion due to windstorms, rain, and flooding is an ongoing danger. Farmers use several techniques to protect the soil. One is to plant rows of crops along the natural curve of a hill. This prevents soil erosion because the

Q8 WHAT'S THE DIFFERENCE BETWEEN PLAINS AND PRAIRIES?

A8 A plain is a large area of fairly flat land. It may or may not have trees and grasses growing on it. *Prairie* comes from the French word for "meadow." A prairie is flat or slightly hilly land covered by grasses and herbs.

crop rows form a series of dams that hold water and keep the soil from washing away. Another technique is to plant rows of short, deep-rooted crops between rows of wheat or corn. The short plants' deep root system helps to hold the soil in place.

In the 1930s, Nebraskans planted long rows of trees as windbreaksto keep soil from blowing away. They also dammed rivers throughout the state to control flooding and provide irrigation water.

Today, state agencies such as the Department of Natural Resources, the Department of Environmental Quality, and the Game and Parks Commission look out for Nebraska's land, air, water, and wildlife. They enforce many laws and regulations to protect the environment. Some laws are designed to keep pesticides and other harmful chemicals from seeping into the underground water sources. Other laws target dump sites for hazardous or toxic wastes. Many other measures are in place to protect wetlands, control air pollution, conserve grazing lands, and assure clean drinking water. They all aim to keep Nebraska clean, beautiful, and productive for years to come.

Rows of trees, acting as windbreaks, edge many farms in Nebraska and help protect the soil.

READ ABOUT

Early inhabitants of Nebraska used spearpoints such as these to hunt animals for food and clothing.

10,000 BCE ▶
Early Nebraskans hunt mammoths and other animals

c. 1000 CE
A culture known as the Village Farmers begins

c. 1400
Most of Nebraska's Native people leave the area

CHAPTER TWO

FIRST PEOPLE

★

FOR CENTURIES, NEBRASKA WAS A CROSSROADS FOR PEOPLE OF MANY CULTURES. Various groups moved in and out of the region. Some were hunters and others were farmers. Some spent their lives moving from place to place. Others settled in villages with thousands of residents. Eventually, the lives of Nebraska's Native people were affected by the growing presence of white and black settlers and fur traders.

Late 1500s

Ancestors of today's Native American groups begin moving into Nebraska

c. 1650 ▲

Native Americans first acquire horses from Spaniards

1700s

Nebraska is home to Pawnees, Omahas, Poncas, Otoes, Sioux, and many other peoples

WORD TO KNOW

game *animals hunted for food*

EARLY NEBRASKA CULTURES

Twelve thousand years ago, North America's last great ice age was coming to an end, and the climate was cool and moist. Mammoths, camels, ground sloths, and early types of horses and bison roamed the land. So did human hunters, constantly following their prey. Their weapons were spears with points chipped from stone. Some spears had long, wooden handles. Other spears had short handles so that hunters could shoot them using a device called an atlatl.

Around 9,000 years ago, Nebraska's climate began to change, and the landscape began to look much as it does today. Swamps and marshy areas dried out, and grassy plains took their place. Water gathered in valleys, creating Nebraska's present-day rivers. Animals that thrived in earlier times became extinct. Change forced people to adapt. They replaced big **game** with smaller animals and wild plants for food.

About 2,000 years ago, early Nebraskans began developing many new ways of life. As their population grew, they came into contact with other peoples. Some of the Nebraskans' new skills originated with people living in the woodlands east of Nebraska. For example, bows and arrows became the new hunting tools. Pottery was another newly adopted skill. People began making large pottery containers for storing and cooking food. For the first time, early Nebraskans began settling in villages. They began small-scale farming, too.

MIGRATIONS

Over the centuries, Nebraska's climate shifted between times of drought and periods of moisture. During droughts, people couldn't raise crops, and wild animal herds left in search of water and grazing land. People

Native American Peoples

(Before European Contact)

This map shows the general area of Native American peoples befores European settlers arrived.

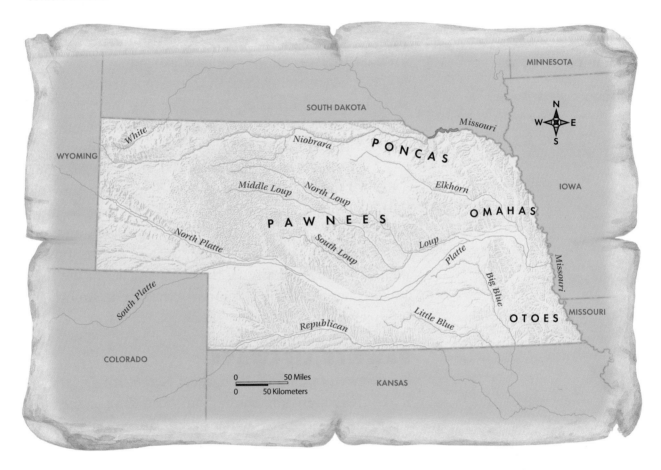

were forced to migrate in search of moist, fertile soil. As the climate changed, various peoples moved into Nebraska, left the area, and moved back in again.

By about 1000 CE, thousands of settlements flourished in eastern Nebraska. People clustered near rivers and streams in permanent villages of as many as a dozen houses. Family homes, called earth lodges, were rectangular with a long entryway. The walls had a framework of wooden poles intertwined with branches, grass, and vines and covered with a mud plaster. People kept tools and extra food in storage pits beneath the floor. They hunted bison with bows and arrows, fished with bone hooks, and gathered wild plants. But for the most part, their daily lives revolved around farming, so **archaeologists** call them Village Farmers.

Village Farmers raised an abundance of corn, beans, squash, and other crops. To till the soil, they used the shoulder blades of bison. After the harvest, people cut corn off the cobs with the sharp jawbones of deer.

As farms grew bigger, so did the villages. But around 1400, Nebraska's Native people began moving away. No one is sure why. Maybe the climate became drier. Or maybe the farms couldn't produce enough to feed the growing population. Just as mysteriously, people began migrating back into Nebraska in the late 1500s. They developed cultures of the Native American groups we know today.

PAWNEE LIFEWAYS

Pawnees were among the earliest Native Americans to make their homes in the region. According to the stories of their origins, Pawnees came from a place that was far southwest of Nebraska, where they had lived in stone houses. This may have been the Antelope Valley region of the Texas Panhandle. Droughts or the arrival of Apache groups may have driven Pawnees from this location.

Arriving in Nebraska in the 1500s, Pawnees settled in what is now the central part of the state. There they set up large villages in the Platte, Republican, and Loup river valleys. Some Pawnee villages had more than 1,000 residents. Pawnees became the largest Native

WORD TO KNOW

archaeologists *people who study the remains of past human societies*

A Pawnee village on the Missouri River

American group in today's Nebraska. By 1800, Nebraska was home to as many as 12,000 Pawnee people.

For Pawnees, the spiritual world was an ever-present force. Their highest **deity** was Tirawa, the creator. Other gods were associated with heavenly bodies, such as the sun, moon, and morning and evening stars. Lesser gods were helpers and protectors. They were linked to animals. Pawnees marked important events with elaborate religious ceremonies. There were rituals for house building, hunting trips, planting and harvest times, and many other occasions.

Pawnee women prepared the food, raised the children, and took care of the farms. Homes were round earthen lodges with floors sunken slightly below the ground. Four large, wooden posts held up the roof beams, and earth covered the roof. The four posts were

WORD TO KNOW

deity *a being regarded as a god*

WORD TO KNOW

equinox *one of the two days of the year when day and night are of equal length*

painted different colors—white, yellow, black, and red—in honor of the four special stars that held up the heavens. Doorways faced east to greet the rising sun on the spring **equinox**. The sun's rays fell upon the household altar on the western wall, which was dedicated to the evening star. Corn and the buffalo, gifts of the evening star, were honored at the altar. A hole in the roof let out smoke from the fireplace beneath it and allowed the residents to view the skies.

Villagers raised corn, beans, squash, pumpkins, and melons in a large community garden surrounding their village. Women dried the corn and beans and stored them in underground pits. People could eat these dried foods during the long, cold winter.

Twice a year, Pawnees left their villages and trekked westward to hunt buffalo across the plains. Once they had horses, they could travel hundreds of miles on hunting expeditions. In hunting camps, each family built a tepee as a temporary home. It was a circle of wooden poles joined at the top and covered with animal hides. Pawnee men hunted not only buffalo but also deer, bears, beavers, raccoons, and squirrels. Some meat the villagers ate right away. The rest they cut into strips, dried, and packed up for winter storage. After the hunt, Pawnees returned to their permanent village homes.

Children learned Pawnee ways from their older relatives. The grandfathers told them traditional Pawnee stories. Girls worked with their mothers, learning to garden, cook, and sew. They also played with dolls and toy tepees. Fathers and uncles taught boys how to make tools and weapons and how to hunt and fight. Boys learned to hunt small game animals such as quail, raccoons, and prairie chickens.

Native Americans had hunted on foot until Spanish explorers introduced horses to North America.

THE HORSE REVOLUTION

Do you walk to school? Do you walk to your friends' and relatives' homes? Do you walk to movies, sports games, and malls? Let's suppose that walking was your only way to get around. Just planning your travel time would be a big concern. Some activities would take all day. Others would be too hard to do at all. Then suppose a big change came over your community. All of a sudden, people had bikes, cars, and public transportation. Your whole way of life would change. You could travel farther than you ever had before, and many new activities would be available to you. That's what it was like when horses arrived on the Great Plains.

Until the 1600s, Nebraska's Native Americans walked almost everywhere. They walked to their hunting grounds, and they traveled on foot when they

THE ALL-PURPOSE ANIMAL

Native Americans respected the buffalo as a spiritual being. They also used nearly every part of a buffalo for food, clothing, shelter, or tools. Little was wasted. The meat, fat, bone marrow, and most internal organs were eaten. Spoons, cups, and rattles were made from the horns. Bones became knives, shovels, hoes, scrapers, paintbrushes, and sled runners. The tendons were made into bowstrings and thread. Raw hides made good shields, drums, saddles, ropes, and snowshoes. Tanned hides became tepee coverings, blankets, moccasins, leggings, robes, and other clothing. The hooves yielded a kind of glue, and even the tails were useful. They were made into whips and flyswatters.

migrated to new home sites. Dogs were their pack animals. Fitted with harnesses, dogs dragged platforms that slid along the ground.

A type of horse had existed in the Americas in earlier times. It had become extinct, probably because of climate changes. Meanwhile horses survived in Asia and Europe. People bred them to produce strong, sturdy pack animals as well as swift runners. Horses were useful for getting places, carrying loads, and sending messages. They were also essential in trade and warfare.

Astride their horses, Spanish explorers first entered the Great Plains in the 1500s. Native Americans had never seen these strange animals before. But by the mid-1600s, they had acquired Spanish horses and were using them. Horses changed their ways of life. Some groups abandoned their settled life of farming. With horses, they could roam the plains and hunt. Traditional hunters could range farther than ever before. Some groups rode their horses long distances to trade with other peoples. In this way, horses spread north to Native Americans in Nebraska.

FARMERS OF EASTERN NEBRASKA

The Native peoples of eastern and central Nebraska were farmers. Omaha and Ponca people were closely related. They migrated from the Ohio and Wabash river valleys, east of the Mississippi River. In the 1700s, they settled along the Missouri River in northeastern Nebraska. They built earth lodges, as Pawnees did, with a smoke hole in the roof. However, they did not attach as much religious meaning to their homes.

Omahas were divided into two groups of clans. The Earth group held ceremonies related to earthly

Omahas, as well as many other Native peoples in Nebraska, lived in earth lodges.

matters such as food and warfare. The Sky group was responsible for ceremonies to gain spiritual aid. Traditional Ponca religion centered on the creator, Wakánda, and on beliefs in the supernatural forces present in all things.

Near their lodges, Omahas and Poncas cleared farming plots. There they raised corn, beans, and squash. Twice a year, they migrated westward to hunt buffalo on the plains. The first trip took place in the summer, after the crops began to grow. The second trip was after the autumn harvest.

Two other groups—Otoes and Missourias—made their homes in eastern Nebraska. Like other Nebraska groups, this was not their original home. In the late 1600s, Otoes lived in present-day Iowa, and Missourias lived in today's Missouri. By the early 1700s, white settlers were moving farther into Otoe territory. So Otoes left Iowa and moved to Nebraska's Platte River valley.

Riding Nebraska's plains on ponies, Sioux hunted buffalo using bows and arrows.

They settled near where the Platte empties into the Missouri River. There they established permanent villages where they farmed for most of the year. Like their neighbors to the north, they built earth lodges and traveled west to hunt twice a year.

Meanwhile, Missourias were quickly dying out. From their contact with white traders, they had caught diseases for which they had no resistance. By the 1790s, there were few Missourias left. Those who survived moved into Nebraska. There they lived among Otoes for safety.

PEOPLES OF THE WESTERN PLAINS

Western Nebraska was home to many groups who lived by hunting buffalo. This included the Lakota Sioux. These people had no permanent villages. Instead, they moved from one hunting site to another, setting up tepees in each new location.

Before the 1700s, Sioux lived across much of the Midwest. They were divided into many separate groups and bands. Teton Sioux, or Teton Lakotas, began moving south and west from the forests of Wisconsin and Minnesota around 1700. Once they acquired horses around 1740, they began migrating across the Great Plains. Seven bands of Teton Sioux moved into western Nebraska—the two largest being Brulé and Oglala.

With horses, Sioux could follow the buffalo herds. The men usually organized a group hunt. Sometimes they drove the animals into an enclosed canyon or over a cliff. At other times, some men surrounded the herd to keep them from stampeding, while others shot the buffalo. Sioux hunted with bows and arrows until the 1800s, when they obtained rifles from settlers and fur traders.

After the hunt, women cut up the buffalo and dried the meat. They also treated the hides so they could be made into clothing, blankets, ropes, and many other useful items. Women took special pride in preparing buffalo hides for tepee coverings, as it was the women who built the tepees at each new hunting camp.

RELIGION, WARFARE, AND VISIONS

For Sioux, every creature and object in the universe was, and is, holy. The spiritual force that flows through everything is called *Wakan Tanka*. This force shows

Picture Yourself . . .

Preparing a Buffalo Hide

Lifting the flap at the entrance to your tepee, you see the hunters return. Today's hunt was a great success, for the buffalo have been generous and kind. They have allowed themselves to be killed so your people can survive. Now your mother's work begins. Today, you will help her prepare the buffalo hides for their many uses.

First, you stretch the hides on the ground, holding them in place with pegs around the edges. Using a sharp buffalo leg bone, you scrape fat and flesh off the hides. Once they dry in the sun, they will be rawhide—a hard, stiff leather. It will make good snowshoes you can wear next winter.

Next, your mother chooses some hides to make into soft leather by tanning them. To do this, you and your mother cook buffalo fat, brains, and liver and make them into a paste. You spread the paste across the hides and leave them to dry in the sun. Your mother will make these soft, flexible hides into new leggings and moccasins for you to wear.

Q: WHAT ARE THE SEVEN SACRED CEREMONIES OF SIOUX?

A: There are different accounts of these ceremonies. Here is one version:

1. The sweat lodge—for purifying the mind and spirit
2. The naming ceremony—for giving a child its name
3. The healing ceremony—for restoring health of mind, body, and spirit
4. The adoption ceremony—for making new relatives; that is, creating a bond between people
5. The marriage ceremony—for uniting a man and a woman
6. The vision quest—for communicating with Wakan Tanka for guidance
7. The Sun Dance—to pray for the welfare of all people

Other accounts include the keeping of the soul (to honor the dead), the coming-of-age ceremony (to prepare a girl for womanhood), and the throwing of the ball (to receive a great blessing).

itself through such things as the sun, Father Sky, Mother Earth, and the four directions. Wakan Tanka also appears through animal messengers and helpers and each person's guardian spirit.

An important spiritual being in the Sioux religion is White Buffalo Calf Woman. She gave the Sioux people a sacred bundle—a pipe wrapped in buffalo hide. Then she taught them how to pray. They were to use the pipe to honor Wakan Tanka in the Seven Sacred Ceremonies.

As the woman left, she turned into a white buffalo calf. Suddenly, a great herd of buffalo appeared. They would give up their lives so that Sioux might live. The buffalo was an especially holy creature, because it provided most of the things Sioux needed.

Because buffalo were so vital to their way of life, Sioux often fought to protect their hunting grounds. So they became known as fierce warriors. A valiant warrior was honored among his people. His brave deeds lived on through storytelling, songs, and special ceremonies.

Young men prepared for warrior life by wandering into the wilderness on what is called a vision quest. Beset by fear, hunger, cold, and sleeplessness, the young man began to have dream visions. Through these visions, Wakan Tanka revealed new truths for the young man to take back to his people.

Both men and women could go off on vision quests. Men sometimes sought visions in the sweat lodge. There they spent days around hot stones or a blazing fire, sweating to become pure, until the visions came. Visions might reveal songs, lessons, or healing cures. They might present solutions to problems. Visions might also reveal the animal whose spirit would give the person strength, guidance, and protection.

By the early 1700s, Nebraska's Native Americans had regular contacts with white explorers and traders. The traders provided valuable trade goods such as iron, tools, weapons, glass beads, and horses. They also brought diseases that killed thousands of Native people. Eventually, the newcomers took Native lands and altered much of their culture.

For Sioux, many activities were marked by ceremonies and worship, as seen below in George Catlin's painting *Sioux Worshipping at the Red Boulders.*

MINI-BIO

ROGER WELSCH: FRIEND OF THE PAWNEE NATION

Roger Welsch (1936—) was already a well-known folklorist, author, and TV journalist when he made national headline news in 2007. At that time, he gave 60 acres of his fertile farmland near the Middle Loup River southeast of Dannebrog to the Pawnee Nation of Oklahoma. It is the first land the Pawnee owned since 1875, when they were forced onto a reservation in Oklahoma. Because of the Pawnee's historic claim to the land, Welsch said it never belonged to him.

? **Want to know more?** Visit www.factsfornow .scholastic.com and enter the keyword **Nebraska**.

READ ABOUT

Nebraska was
sometimes a
gathering place for
trappers, traders,
and buyers
to meet and
exchange furs and
goods.

1714

*French explorer Étienne
de Véniard, Sieur de
Bourgmont, is the first
European to reach
Nebraska*

▲1720

*Pawnees and Otoes defeat
Spanish troops near the fork
of the Loup and Platte rivers*

1739

*French fur traders
Pierre and Paul Mallet
cross Nebraska*

CHAPTER THREE

EXPLORATION AND SETTLEMENT

★

ENGLISH COLONIES WERE BEING CREATED ON THE ATLANTIC COAST IN THE 1600S. In time, English settlers would reach present-day Nebraska. Meanwhile, Spain and France ignored England's claim to the land and explored the continent as they pleased. However, Native Americans already lived in this region. The European newcomers had various ways of dealing with the Indians they met.

1754

The French and Indian War begins

1763

The French and Indian War ends; Nebraska passes from French to Spanish rule

United States, 1803
United States Territory, 1803
Louisiana Purchase
Present-day state of Nebraska

◄1803

Nebraska is part of the Louisiana Purchase

EXPLORER, TRADER, AND DEAL MAKER

Étienne de Véniard, Sieur de Bourgmont (1679–1734), spent many years exploring North America. He was the first European to map the Missouri and Platte rivers. In Missouri territory, he fell in love with the daughter of a Missouria chief. He moved into her village, and they married and had a son. On one of Bourgmont's explorations, he met Nebraska's Otoes at the Platte River. Later, he traveled across the plains making trade treaties with Indian groups. After many more explorations, he retired to France, where he died.

In 1725, an Otoe man and other Native Americans were taken to France to meet the king. One visitor said the perfumed French ladies "smelled like alligators!"

TRADING FRIENDSHIP FOR FURS

The first European to reach Nebraska was Étienne de Véniard, Sieur de Bourgmont. He was a French explorer, trader, and soldier. France had sent him to explore North America and meet with the Native people. He sought to make friends and gain the right to the fur trade in their territories.

In 1714, Bourgmont sailed up the Missouri as far as the mouth of the Platte River. There he met Otoes and made the trading deals he wanted. The French would provide Native Americans with guns, gunpowder, and other goods. In return, the Indians would provide beaver pelts and other animal skins. Soon, many French fur traders and trappers were venturing into Nebraska.

A SPANISH DEFEAT

French explorations made the Spaniards nervous. Although they had never set foot in Nebraska, they had claimed it, and so they said the French were trespassing. What was worse, the French were reaping huge profits from the fur trade. Spain decided to defend its claims. In 1720, Spanish soldiers under Pedro de Villasur marched out of Santa Fe, in today's New Mexico. Their destination? Nebraska. Their mission? To put an end to the French fur trade.

Villasur and his men reached the Platte River. After crossing it, they camped in a meadow by the Loup River, near present-day Columbus. By this time, Pawnees and Otoes were allies of the French. While the Spaniards were sleeping, the Indians attacked. French fur traders also may have joined them. By the time the battle was over, 35 Spaniards lay dead, including Villasur.

JOSÉ LOPEZ NARANJO: FRONTIERSMAN AND SCOUT

José Lopez Naranjo (?–1720) was a New Mexican Pueblo Indian serving as a captain under the Spanish army. As a skilled frontiersman and guide, Naranjo led the Spaniards on many expeditions through the Spanish territories. He was the chief scout on Pedro de Villasur's 1720 expedition into Nebraska. Naranjo was one of the dozens of people killed in the battle with Pawnees.

This buffalo hide painting depicts the defeat of the Spanish by Pawnees and the French in Nebraska in 1720.

The French continued with their fur-trading ventures. In 1739, two brothers, Pierre and Paul Mallet, crossed almost the entire width of Nebraska, trading with Pawnees for furs.

WARS AND SHIFTING POWER

Meanwhile, English settlers were pushing westward from the Atlantic coast. As they moved deeper into the continent's interior, they clashed with French traders and settlers. This conflict exploded into what is called the French and Indian War (1754–1763). This war in North America was part of a larger war in Europe—the Seven Years' War. It ended with a drastic shift in power.

France had been a great power in North America. It had controlled Canada and the vast American Midwest, which it called Louisiana. After the war, however, France lost all its North American holdings. Great Britain took Canada and all lands east of the Mississippi River. France's bitter rival,

SEE IT HERE!

HISTORY RECORDED ON HIDES

An unknown artist—either Indian or Spanish—made a painting of Villasur's battle on stitched-together buffalo hides. You can see a replica of that painting on cowhides in the Nebraska State Historical Society Museum in Lincoln. The detailed battle scene provides vivid depictions of Pawnee body painting and French and Spanish uniforms and weapons.

Spain, took the territory west of the Mississippi—which included Nebraska. However, French fur traders still kept up their business in Nebraska.

Another big shift in power was about to take place in the East. Colonists along the Atlantic coast had had enough of Great Britain's tyrannical rule. To gain their freedom,

Exploration of Nebraska

The colored arrows on this map show the routes taken by explorers and pioneers between 1804 and 1844.

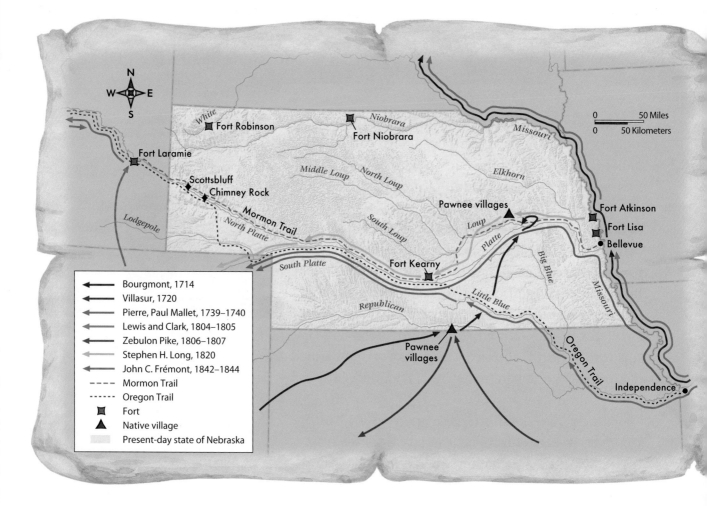

Louisiana Purchase

This map shows the area (in yellow) that made up the Louisiana Purchase and the present-day state of Nebraska (in orange).

Louisiana Purchase

British Possessions

Spanish Possessions

N W E S

United States, 1803

United States Territory, 1803

Louisiana Purchase

Present-day state of Nebraska

OWNING THE TERRITORY

Nebraska quickly changed hands, from Spain to France to the United States. In a secret agreement, Spain returned the Louisiana Territory to France in 1800. But in 1803, France sold the entire Louisiana Territory to the United States in a deal called the Louisiana Purchase.

The United States agreed to purchase the Louisiana Territory for $15 million. That's less than 3 cents per acre (7 cents per ha)!

Q8 WHAT LANDS WERE INCLUDED IN FRANCE'S LOUISIANA TERRITORY?

A8 Louisiana Territory included all of present-day Arkansas, Missouri, Iowa, Oklahoma, Kansas, and Nebraska and parts of Minnesota, North Dakota, South Dakota, New Mexico, Texas, Montana, Wyoming, Colorado, and Louisiana.

they fought the American Revolution (1775–1783). In 1776, Americans issued their Declaration of Independence. It declared the colonies were a free nation.

In 1789, the new United States drew up the basic principles of its new government in the U.S. Constitution. The new nation would not have a king. Instead, it would have a president and other leaders elected by the people. Nebraska eventually would join this union.

READ ABOUT

Meriwether Lewis
and William Clark
were guided by
Sacagawea on
their expedition.

1804

*Meriwether Lewis and
William Clark explore
eastern Nebraska and meet
with Native Americans at
Council Bluff*

1823

*Bellevue becomes Nebraska's
first permanent white
settlement*

▲ 1843

*Pioneers begin taking
the Oregon Trail across
Nebraska*

CHAPTER FOUR

GROWTH AND CHANGE

★

IN 1804, U.S. PRESIDENT THOMAS JEFFERSON SENT AN EXPEDITION TO THE LOUISIANA TERRITORY, WHICH HAD BEEN PURCHASED IN 1803. The expedition was led by Meriwether Lewis and William Clark. They were to draw maps, list plants and animals, and meet with Native people and take notes about their cultures.

1854
*Congress establishes
Nebraska Territory*

1862
*The Homestead Act
offers free land to
settlers in Nebraska*

1867 ►
*Nebraska becomes
the 37th U.S. state*

AMERICAN EXPLORERS, TRADERS, AND SETTLEMENTS

Lewis and Clark, heading up the Missouri River, reached present-day Nebraska in July 1804 and explored its eastern edge. Just north of the Platte River, they reached a point they called Council Bluff, near today's Fort Calhoun. There they met with Otoe and Missouria chiefs.

The explorers' reports sparked enormous interest of fur traders and the U.S. Army. Lieutenant Zebulon Pike explored the region for the army in 1806. In 1812, the Spanish-American trader Manuel Lisa set up a trading post called Fort Lisa. It was located near the spot where Lewis and Clark had met with Native Americans. The army established Fort Atkinson at that same place in 1819. Its goal was to protect whites from Native Americans who resented the invasion.

In 1820, Major Stephen Long explored the Great Plains. In Nebraska, he traveled along the Platte River, where he met with Pawnees and Otoes. Long called this region the Great American Desert, saying it was "almost wholly unfit for cultivation"!

The town of Bellevue, along the Missouri River, was founded in 1823 as a fur-trading post by the Missouri Fur Company. It was Nebraska's first permanent white settlement. By this time, people were following the Platte River to cross Nebraska. In 1830, a wagon train of fur traders took the Platte River valley to reach the Rocky Mountains. This would become the standard route for future wagon trains.

THE GREAT MIGRATION

In the 1840s, thousands of pioneers from the eastern United States began heading west. They hoped to find a better life in the wide-open western territories. They

This 1869 oil painting by Albert Bierstadt depicts a westward-bound group of settlers.

crossed Nebraska along well-traveled trails. This mass movement of pioneers is called the Great Migration.

The first trail to open was the Oregon Trail. In 1843, the U.S. Congress passed a law allowing people to settle in Oregon. Setting out from Independence, Missouri, pioneers headed west in their covered wagons. Their trip took four to six months.

Another group of pioneers who headed west were Mormons—members of the Church of Jesus Christ of Latter-day Saints. To escape religious persecution, more than 3,000 Mormons left Nauvoo, Illinois, in 1846. They were bound for Utah, where they could settle and enjoy religious freedom. After stopping for the winter in Florence (now a part of Omaha), they continued west along what is called the Mormon Trail.

Picture Yourself...

in a Wagon Train on the Oregon Trail

It's five o'clock in the morning, and you're ready to start your day. You yawn, brush the dirt off your clothes, and then wander out to collect buffalo chips. These dried buffalo droppings aren't as good a fuel as wood. But many travelers have passed this way before, and there are few trees left for firewood.

Once the campfire is blazing, you help your mother fix breakfast. Most mornings, that's biscuits, bacon, and coffee. Baking bread outdoors has its drawbacks. As you bite into your biscuit, your teeth crunch on bugs and dirt.

After breakfast, you help yoke the oxen to the wagon and hit the trail. Everyone stops for lunch around noon. The menu's no surprise. It's bread and bacon again. As the sun goes down, you stop to camp for the night. Soon the fires are lit, and dinner is on its way. If you're lucky, someone has bagged an antelope, a buffalo, or some quail. Otherwise, the menu is the same as it's been all day.

By the firelight, some people tell stories. Others sing songs to the tune of a fiddle or an accordion. By 9:00 P.M., everyone is worn out. You find a level spot on the ground that's not too rocky. Then you curl up and drift off to sleep under the starry sky.

At first, only a few wagon trains rumbled along these trails. But in 1848, gold was discovered in California. This brought on a rush of westward-bound travelers. They followed the California Trail to the goldfields.

Along the trail, pioneers passed huge rock formations. They gazed in awe at Courthouse Rock and Jail Rock near Bridgeport and at the tall, pointy spire of Chimney Rock near Bayard. But Scottsbluff, near Gering, was a massive obstacle for travelers. Some pioneers went south to avoid this huge rock formation. Then travelers found a route through the bluff at Mitchell Pass. As hundreds of wagons passed through, their wheels cut deep ruts in the soft stone.

Chimney Rock, Nebraska

CROSSING THE HUNTING GROUNDS

During their westward trek, pioneers and Native Americans often had friendly relations. Indians helped dig out stuck wagons, save drowning travelers, and round up lost cattle. But in western Nebraska, Native Americans considered the pioneers unwelcome and dangerous. Pioneers used up the available firewood. Their livestock trampled and overgrazed the grasslands where buffalo, antelope, and other game animals grazed. Pioneers shot buffalo and other animals for food.

As the pioneers stripped traditional Native American hunting grounds, some Indian groups were beginning to go hungry. Fighting for survival, the Native people sometimes attacked the wagon trains. In 1848, the U.S. Army opened Fort Kearny to protect westbound settlers. The fort stood just outside today's city of Kearney.

In the interest of peace, a diplomatic meeting was held in 1851 at Fort Laramie, in present-day Wyoming. Leaders of Brulé and Oglala Sioux and several other groups attended. With U.S. representatives, they signed the Fort Laramie Treaty. In this agreement, each Indian group was assigned a territory. The Indians agreed to let travelers along the Platte River pass through unharmed. In return, the United States pledged that the Native Americans would possess their assigned lands forever. The United States also agreed to pay the Indians $50,000 worth of trade goods every year for 50 years.

What went wrong with the Fort Laramie Treaty? Native Americans who signed the treaty were not the legal Native leaders. They did not have the authority to make an agreement. The U.S. representatives did

SEE IT HERE!

LIFE ON THE TRAIL

Covered wagons rumble along, thunder crashes, lightning flashes, and herds of buffalo go stampeding by. That's what it's like at the Great Platte River Road Archway Monument. This museum in Kearney is a memorial to all the pioneers who passed along the westward trails. Its exhibits place you in the middle of the action as you experience life on the trail.

FAQ

Q8 WHAT LANDS WERE INCLUDED IN NEBRASKA TERRITORY?

A8 Nebraska Territory was much bigger than today's state of Nebraska. It was a vast region that extended all the way up to the Canadian border. Nebraska Territory covered all of present-day Nebraska, as well as parts of North Dakota, South Dakota, Montana, Wyoming, and Colorado.

not provide what they promised. The U.S. Congress changed the terms from 50 years to 10 years, without informing the Native Americans. Misunderstandings, resentments, and violations eventually made the treaty worthless. Oglala chief Red Cloud later led a resistance movement called Red Cloud's War. It led to the Fort Laramie Treaty of 1868, which created a Sioux reservation in South Dakota.

NEBRASKA TERRITORY AND THE SODBUSTERS

Bitter debates over slavery divided Congress in the 1800s. The Missouri Compromise of 1820 had provided that there would be no slavery in new western territories. But the Kansas-Nebraska Act in 1854, which established the Nebraska Territory, changed that. It allowed people in the new territories of Kansas and Nebraska to choose whether they wanted slavery or not. The act brought violence to Kansas, which exploded into its own civil war

Family members pose outside their sod home in the late 1880s.

several years before the American Civil War began. However, Nebraska proceeded peacefully to become a state that rejected slavery. In 1860, Nebraska had 63 Africans, and 15 were enslaved. In 1861, the territorial **legislature** abolished slavery.

Once Nebraska became a territory, the U.S. government opened the land for settlement, disregarding Nebraska's Native Americans. In 1854, it forced Otoes and Missourias living in eastern Nebraska, south of the Platte River, to move to a reservation near the Kansas border. Eventually, the U.S. government forced Otoes, Missourias, and Pawnees to relocate to Oklahoma.

In 1876, Standing Bear, a Ponca chief, stood before a U.S. district court judge in Fort Omaha and demanded the right of his people to return to their homelands in Nebraska. A U.S. judge officially ruled for the first time that Native Americans were persons. Standing Bear and his Ponca nation gained the right to leave their reservation in the Indian Territory and return to Nebraska.

The United States had passed the Homestead Act in 1862. It granted 160 acres (65 ha) of free land to anyone who settled on it for five years, unleashing a flood of white settlers. With few trees for wood, many settlers built **sod** houses. They dug up chunks of sod and used it to make the roofs and walls. Settlers on the Great Plains were sometimes called sodbusters.

MINI-BIO

DANIEL FREEMAN: THE EARLY BIRD GETS THE FARM

Daniel Freeman (1826–1908) wanted a plot of land near Beatrice, Nebraska. He knew the Homestead Act would go into effect at midnight on New Year's Day, January 1, 1863. On New Year's Eve, he ran into the clerk for the local land office. Freeman talked him into opening the office a few minutes after midnight. Then Freeman filed his claim, becoming the first person to claim land under the Homestead Act. Freeman's farm is now the Homestead National Monument of America.

? Want to know more? Visit www.factsfornow.scholastic.com and enter the keyword **Nebraska**.

WORDS TO KNOW

legislature the lawmaking body of a state, country, or other political unit

sod soil thickly packed together with grass and roots

Nebraska: From Territory to Statehood
(1854–1867)

This map shows the original Nebraska territory and the area (outlined in red) that became the state of Nebraska in 1867.

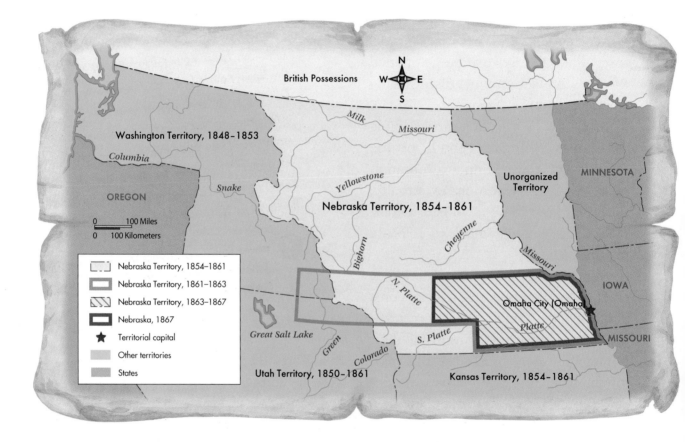

NEW WAYS TO CROSS NEBRASKA

Pioneer wagon trains weren't the only vehicles on the Platte River route across Nebraska. The 1850s and 1860s were the glory days of stagecoach travel. Heading west from Missouri, the coaches rumbled through Omaha and on to California, stopping at towns along the way. About every 15 miles (24 km), a coach stopped at a station, called a stage, for a fresh team of horses. Stagecoaches carried passengers, cargo, mail, and sometimes chests of money. For the passengers, it was a bumpy, rickety ride—a combination of excitement and danger. Though they enjoyed magnificent scenery, they risked run ins with gun wielding bandits and Native Americans protecting their lands.

The Pony Express was launched in 1860. Its riders raced across mountains and plains carrying mail between California and Missouri. Their route across Nebraska was the old, reliable Platte River valley. The Pony Express lasted only about 18 months, because people found a new way to send messages.

Workers completed the nation's first extensive telegraph line in 1861, forcing the 18-month-old Pony Express out of business.

WORD TO KNOW

transcontinental *crossing an entire continent*

FAQ

Q: HOW FAST COULD PEOPLE SEND MESSAGES IN THE 1800S?

A: Suppose you sent a letter by ship from San Francisco, California, to New York City. That letter arrived in about 45 days. Traveling on a stagecoach, a letter from San Francisco to St. Louis, Missouri, would arrive in about 20 days. By Pony Express, mail got from Sacramento, California, to St. Joseph, Missouri, in 11 days. But a message sent by telegraph took only a few minutes.

In 1861, workers completed the nation's first **transcontinental** telegraph line. It stretched from Omaha to Carson City, Nevada, linking the western and eastern United States. Across Nebraska's plains, the Western Union Telegraph Company put up telegraph poles and strung hundreds of miles of telegraph wires. With lightning-quick speed, the telegraph created a revolution in communications. It could send messages so fast that the volume of paper mail dropped off dramatically.

THE TRANSCONTINENTAL RAILROAD

A transportation revolution began with the transcontinental railroad. With coast-to-coast tracks, it linked railroads in the eastern United States with the West Coast. Omaha was as far as the eastern railroads ran. So the Union Pacific Railroad built tracks westward from its headquarters in Omaha. Meanwhile, the Central Pacific Railroad built tracks eastward from California. The two rail lines would meet in Utah.

Naturally, the railroad followed the Platte River valley. Construction through eastern Nebraska went fairly quickly. It began in 1865, and the tracks reached Fort Kearny in 1866. But once the construction crews reached Nebraska's western plains, Native Americans were outraged. The railroad violated their treaties with the United States.

Worse still, the railroad workers shot thousands of sacred buffalo. Partly, they wanted the meat and hides. Partly, they thought shooting buffalo was fun. But they also hoped to wipe out the Indians' way of life. If they destroyed the buffalo herds, Indians would lose the mainstay of their existence. Of course, this led to bitter

battles. Nevertheless, the transcontinental railroad was completed in 1869. Soon cattle-raising operations grew up around the railway lines. More distant ranchers drove their herds in great cattle drives to the main railroad towns, where they could ship their cattle to faraway markets by train.

The construction of the transcontinental railroad sped the opening of the West for settlement.

MINI-BIO

SUSAN LAFLESCHE PICOTTE: HEALER TO HER PEOPLE

Susan Laflesche Picotte (1865–1915) was the first Native American woman to earn a medical degree. Born on the Omaha Reservation in northeastern Nebraska, she received her medical training in Philadelphia, Pennsylvania. Then she returned to provide medical care for her people and helped them adjust to life in the non-Indian world. Her dream was for the reservation to have a hospital, and the Dr. Susan Picotte Memorial Hospital opened in Walthill in 1913.

? Want to know more? Visit www.factsfornow .scholastic.com and enter the keyword **Nebraska**.

Both the state of Nebraska and Peru State College, Nebraska's oldest institution for higher education, celebrate their 150th anniversaries in 2017.

THE NEW STATE

After the railroad was built, the Union Pacific Railroad tried to get more people to move to Nebraska. New settlers would mean more people paying to ride trains. Railroad agents advertised in the eastern United States and even in Europe. Nebraska, they said, was a Garden of Eden. That brought in another wave of settlers. With its growing population, Nebraska was ready for statehood.

As required, Nebraskans established a lawmaking body, drew up a state constitution, and held a vote for approval of statehood. On March 1, 1867, Congress made Nebraska the 37th U.S. state. Not all settlers had a say in its government, though. Nebraska had abolished slavery before the Civil War, but it still denied the vote to nonwhites, as well as all women, when it entered the Union. In 1885, Nebraska finally passed a civil rights law that prohibited racial discrimination in public places such as inns, restaurants, trains, barber shops, and theaters.

PIONEERS AND COWBOYS

For pioneers who established farms in Nebraska, life was hard. Shelter was an immediate problem when arriving at a farm site. Many settlers dug into a hillside to create a cramped space where they could live temporarily. With no lumber or bricks for building, settlers often built sod houses, or "soddies," with dirt floors. With frequent thunderstorms and blizzards bombarding them, the soddies often leaked, and snakes and mice could easily crawl in. Just finding water was a major challenge, too. Farm sites by the rivers were taken early, so most settlers had to dig their own wells for water. Then they had to haul the water up one bucketful at a time.

Farmers were getting lower and lower prices for their products. Many blamed the railroads, which were charging high rates to ship goods. To protect their interests, Nebraska farmers banded together in politically active groups. In 1872, they formed the Grange, a cooperative organization through which they could buy low-cost machinery and supplies. The Grange also got the state to regulate the railroads.

In the 1870s, millions of grasshoppers swarmed across Nebraska's farmland and ate people's crops. Hundreds of farm families left the state. New farmers moved in, but drought wiped out their crops in the 1880s. As prices continued to drop, the Farmers Alliance was organized in the 1880s. Farmers were desperate, and the alliance called for drastic measures such as low taxes, a forced price hike, and government ownership of railroads and telegraphs. This led to the formation of the Populist Party, which was able to push through many projects the farmers favored. Thanks to new irrigation projects in the 1890s, Nebraska gradually began to be known as a great place to farm.

Western Nebraska turned out to be best suited for grazing cattle. Ogallala became Nebraska's cowboy capital. It was the end of the Western, or Texas, Trail, a cattle-drive route from Texas. Cowboys herded thousands of cattle to the railroad depot in Ogallala. Before heading back to Texas, the cowboys rested in the wild town—and often got into gunfights, too. Meanwhile, Omaha was growing fast as a center for the meatpacking industry.

THE EXODUSTERS

In 1860, fewer than 70 black people lived in Nebraska. But after the Civil War, African Americans joined the great westward migration. Between 1879 and 1881, thousands of former slaves left the South to set up homesteads on the Great Plains. They were called the Exodusters. That name comes from the Bible's book of Exodus. It tells about the Israelites, who left a life of slavery for the Promised Land. To America's former slaves, the West seemed a promised land as well. Exodusters settled in Oklahoma, Kansas, Nebraska, and Colorado. In Nebraska, some farmed on the western plains, while others settled in Lincoln, Omaha, and other cities.

A picnic in Lincoln around 1920

IMMIGRANTS AND AFRICAN AMERICANS

By this time, thousands of European immigrants and African Americans were pouring into Nebraska in search of better lives. Those from Europe included people from Germany, Norway, Sweden, Switzerland, Ireland, Italy, and Bohemia, a region that is now part of the Czech Republic. In 1870, one-quarter of Nebraska's population had been born in a foreign country. Many former slaves made homes in Nebraska, too. By 1890, Nebraska's black population had reached 8,900. All these pioneers helped build up the state and enrich its culture.

Omaha communities had become mixed by the 1870s and 1880s. A black resident of Omaha reported "Swedish, Bohemian, Italian, Irish and Negro children" playing together. By 1900, about half the white population had been born in Europe, or had a parent who had, and by 1920 the figure was at 40 percent.

During World War I (1914–1918), the black population in Lincoln and Omaha doubled. Racial tensions rose in 1919. A riot against African Americans in Omaha was triggered by disturbances in two dozen other cities caused by job shortages. Segregation was the rule in Omaha and Lincoln.

CHANGING TIMES

The early 1900s brought a new revolution in transportation—automobiles! Dirt trails would no longer work for overland travelers. They needed paved roads. In 1915, the Lincoln Highway was completed through Nebraska. This was the nation's first paved transcontinental highway. It, too, followed the pioneers' pathway along the Platte River. Today, that route is U.S. Route 30 and parts of Interstate 80.

Meanwhile, Nebraska's women were carrying on their own revolution: they wanted the right to vote. Elsewhere in the nation, women began forming organizations for woman suffrage, or voting rights, in the 1840s. In 1871, when Nebraska was drawing up a new constitution, a proposal to include women's voting rights was submitted to Nebraska voters, but it failed. Suffrage measures were defeated again in 1882 and 1914.

Finally, a 1917 law allowed Nebraska women to vote in city elections and for presidential electors. It was a major breakthrough, but it didn't go far enough. Only in 1919 did Nebraska's women get full voting rights. That's when the U.S. Congress passed the 19th Amendment to the U.S. Constitution. At last, Nebraska's hardworking women gained the privilege of voting on matters that affected their own lives.

READ ABOUT

Deep grooves
mark a Nebraska
field in 1936.

1937

Nebraska's unicameral
legislature meets for
the first time

▲ 1948

Offutt Air Force Base
in Bellevue becomes the
headquarters for the
Strategic Air Command
(SAC)

1960

Nebraska's urban
population outnumbers
its rural residents

CHAPTER FIVE

MORE MODERN TIMES

★

AS THE 20TH CENTURY UNFOLDED, NEBRASKANS HAD THEIR SHARE OF GOOD TIMES AND BAD TIMES. In 1929, the nation plunged into the Great Depression, a period of economic hard times. In Nebraska, crop prices fell to an all-time low. Over the next several decades, Nebraskans faced farming disasters, war, upheavals in state government, and a richer economy than they had ever enjoyed before.

◄ **1965**
Omaha native
Malcolm X is
assassinated in
New York City

1982
Initiative 300 bars large
corporations from buying
Nebraska farmland

2012
Nebraska experiences
the driest summer in
state history

Men used plows and horses while building a dam in Nebraska around 1936.

THE DUST BOWL

As Nebraskans were still reeling from the Depression, along came the Dust Bowl. This years-long dry spell devastated the Great Plains. A series of droughts turned farmland to dust, and crops shriveled. As high winds swept across the plains, rich topsoil blew away. Thousands of farm families simply packed up and left. During the 1930s, for the first time ever, Nebraska's population shrank.

Nebraska's U.S. senator George Norris did a lot to help his state during this time. In 1933, he helped create the Tennessee Valley Authority (TVA). This program built dams to control flooding and bring irrigation water to farms. Flooding became a problem when it did rain, as there was little vegetation on the plains to stop the water flow. The TVA provided jobs for many Nebraskans who were unemployed. Norris also made big changes in Nebraska's state government. To cut expenses, he convinced the state legislature, or lawmaking body, to change from two houses of representatives to one. The new unicameral, or one-house, legislature first met in 1937.

At least one good thing came out of the Dust Bowl disaster. People realized the state had to practice soil conservation. One way to protect the soil is to plant more trees. Trees help anchor the soil in place so it doesn't blow away. Long rows of trees called windbreaks helped, too. They slowed the force of high winds, leaving the soil intact. Nebraskans planted millions of windbreak trees in the 1930s.

WARTIME NEBRASKA

World War II (1939–1945) helped pull Nebraska out of its slump. Across the state, farms and factories increased their production. Tons of Nebraska corn, wheat, and beef were shipped overseas to feed U.S. troops. Industrial plants produced ammunition, tanks, bombers, and other equipment. Thousands of Nebraska women joined the workforce as men went off to war.

Ordinary citizens pitched in to help the war effort, too. Many people planted so-called Victory Gardens—backyard vegetable gardens where people grew food for their own families. The big farms were responsible for feeding the troops. Nebraskans also collected scrap metal and paper. These were recycled and made into war supplies.

After U.S. troops captured German soldiers and held them as prisoners of war (POWs), Nebraska's Fort Robinson, Scottsbluff, and many other sites served as prison camps for German POWs. They were held there until the war was over.

MINI-BIO

BEN KUROKI: JAPANESE AMERICAN WAR HERO

Ben Kuroki (1917–) is a war hero and journalist. During World War II, he joined the U.S. Army Air Corps and flew 58 missions as a tail gunner. After the war, he toured the nation campaigning against prejudice toward Japanese Americans, which had peaked during World War II. Then he earned a journalism degree and, in 1950, founded the York [Nebraska] Republican newspaper. In 2005, Kuroki was awarded the U.S. Army Distinguished Service Medal. He was born in Gothenburg.

❓ **Want to know more?** Visit www.factsfornow.scholastic.com and enter the keyword **Nebraska**.

In the 1930s, Nebraskans planted almost 4,170 miles (6,710 km) of trees as part of the Prairie States Forestry Project for soil conservation!

During World War II, women were called to duty to work in factories supporting the war effort.

Q8 WHAT WAS THE SOVIET UNION?

A8 The Soviet Union was a large country that spread from eastern Europe all the way across Asia. In 1991, it broke apart into several smaller countries, including Russia.

POSTWAR PROSPERITY

After the war, the United States and the Soviet Union became rivals in a conflict known as the cold war. Fearful of the Soviets' nuclear weapons, the United States established the Strategic Air Command (SAC) to manage American nuclear defenses. In 1948, the SAC moved to Offutt Air Force Base in Bellevue, near Omaha. Later, SAC's name was changed to the U.S. Strategic Command, or USSTRATCOM.

Nebraska's postwar economy was stronger than ever. The SAC provided jobs and upgraded the region's communications systems. Big Nebraska corporations such as ConAgra, Mutual of Omaha, and the Union Pacific Railroad were thriving. New dams controlled the Missouri and Platte rivers. They provided flood control, irrigation, and hydroelectric power. The dams improved the lives of rural Nebraskans—especially farmers. Nevertheless, people continued to leave their farms for city jobs. By 1960, more Nebraskans lived in cities and towns than in rural areas.

Record numbers of women were taking jobs outside their homes, too. During the war, women had proved their worth as employees, and in the 1960s and 1970s, massive numbers of women entered the workforce. By the 21st century, Nebraska was one of the top-ranking states for the percentage of women in the labor force, and women-owned businesses were the fastest-growing segment of the business community.

CIVIL RIGHTS STRUGGLES

In spite of the state's prosperity, Nebraska's African Americans still had to struggle for equal rights. Black soldiers, who had fought side by side with whites, returned from World War II with less tolerance for America's racist attitude. By 1946, Gordon Lippitt of the Lincoln Urban League led demonstrations to integrate the city's restaurants, swimming pools, housing, and sports events.

In Omaha, the Urban League used boycotts to force the school system to hire African American teachers. Many other civil rights organizations were formed in the 1950s and 1960s. They worked for equal housing, education, and employment rights in the Omaha area and statewide.

FAQ

Q: HOW MANY NEBRASKANS SERVED IN WORLD WAR II?

A: A total of 139,754 Nebraska men and women served in the war.

MINI-BIO

MALCOLM X: CIVIL RIGHTS ACTIVIST

Malcolm X (1925–1965) was an Omaha-born activist in the civil rights movement of the 1960s. Born Malcolm Little, he changed his surname to X in 1952, rejecting the name his ancestors had been given under slavery. The X also stood for his lost history as an African. As a minister in the Nation of Islam, he preached in favor of equal human rights for African Americans. Malcolm X was assassinated in New York City on February 27, 1965.

? **Want to know more?** Visit www.factsfornow.scholastic.com and enter the keyword **Nebraska**.

MINI-BIO

MILDRED BROWN: SPREADING THE GOOD WORD

Mildred Brown (1915–1989) founded the Omaha Star in 1938. It became one of the most successful African American newspapers in the country. Brown made a point of reporting positive news stories about people in Omaha's black community. She also used her newspaper to campaign for racial equality. She gave jobs to many young black people and encouraged them to get an education. She even gave scholarships to those who wanted to go to college.

❓ **Want to know more?** Visit www.factsfornow .scholastic.com and enter the keyword **Nebraska**.

In 1966, violence erupted all over the country, including Omaha. An African American barber named Ernest Chambers became Nebraska's leading spokesman for civil rights. Chambers justified the riots of the 1960s as revolts against discrimination and a part of the American tradition that overthrew tyranny in 1776. He won election to the state legislature in 1970, but left office in 2008 because a new law prevented senators from serving more than two consecutive terms. After sitting out for one four-year term, he was reelected in 2012.

THE FARM CRISIS

In the 1970s, many Nebraska farmers took bank loans to modernize their farms and buy newly developed farm equipment. Then, the early 1980s brought the worst economic disaster Nebraska had seen in 50 years. Crop prices took a nosedive, and so did the value of farmland. In addition, U.S. exports of food to foreign countries dropped. As a result, thousands of Nebraska farmers did not earn enough money to make payments on their loans, and they lost their land.

Still, Nebraska found a way to help. In farming states across the country, giant corporations were buying up farmland. Small family farms were going out of business. Nebraskans were determined that this wouldn't happen to them. In 1982, voters approved Initiative 300. It barred big companies from buying farms or ranches in Nebraska.

RISING UP STRONG

As prices began to rise again in the late 1980s, farm life began to recover. The average farm income rose more than 10 percent between 1989 and the mid-1990s. Fewer people were farming, but the state had larger and more modernized farms. Agriculture also provided the basis for other Nebraska industries. Food plants, trucking companies, and railroads became busy processing and transporting farm products.

The growth of small industries and tourism contributed to Nebraska's bustling economy in the 1990s. Tax laws were passed that made it more attractive for big companies to do business in the state. This kept large employers around that would continue hiring people. By 1999, Nebraska had one of the lowest unemployment rates in the nation, only 2.9 percent.

The worldwide economic crisis of 2007 to 2009 hit Nebraska hard. More than 33,000 jobs were lost during that time. But since 2010, most industries have bounced back. Manufacturing, construction, and transportation are making steady gains, and the state economy has grown stronger each year. Nebraskans have high hopes for the years ahead.

Mountain bikers explore Chadron State Park.

READ ABOUT

The Omaha
Summer Arts
Festival draws
large crowds
annually.

CHAPTER SIX

PEPLE

★

NEBRASKANS ARE PROUD OF THEIR ROOTS. Many share a pioneer background, and they have ancestors from all over the world. Through music, literature, art, and centuries-old traditions, Nebraskans honor their diverse cultures. They know how to have fun, too. From Cornhuskers football to Wild West rodeos to Native American powwows, they celebrate what it means to be a Nebraskan.

LIVING IN NEBRASKA

When it comes to population, Nebraska is a medium-sized state. In 2010, its population was about 1,826,341, making it the 38th-largest state in terms of population.

In the 1800s, almost everyone in Nebraska lived in rural areas, outside of the big population centers. They were farming across the wide-open prairies. But farm life has dwindled drastically since then. Year after year, more Nebraskans have left their farms for job opportunities in cities and towns. Rural towns have been getting smaller, too. Almost 90 percent of Nebraska's cities have populations under 3,000 people. And hundreds of towns are home to fewer than 1,000 residents.

In 2010, three counties in eastern Nebraska—Douglas, Lancaster, and Sarpy—accounted for 54 percent of the state's entire population. Because of that, the state's three congressional districts had to be reorganized. The large Third Congressional District shifted farther east to pick up more population. U.S. congressman Adrian Smith must now serve a district that covers about 65,000 square miles (168,000 sq km) and stretches into two time zones.

ETHNIC GROUPS

The majority of Nebraskans are white people with European ancestors. They make up 82 percent of the population. Hispanic people and African Americans make up the next-largest ethnic groups. Many Mexican people settled in Scottsbluff to work in the sugar beet fields. People of Mexican heritage also live in Grand Island, Lincoln, and Omaha. Most of Nebraska's African Americans live in the Omaha area. Thousands of Asian Americans and Native Americans make their homes in Nebraska, too.

Big City Life

This list shows the population of Nebraska's biggest cities.

Omaha 408,958
Lincoln 258,378
Bellevue 50,137
Grand Island 48,520
Kearney 30,787

Source: U.S. Census Bureau, 2010 census

Butler County is one of only two counties in the nation where Czech Americans make up a majority of the population.

Omaha is also home to the United States' largest community of refugees from the country of Sudan. The Sudanese population in Omaha has grown from 1,200 in 1998 to more than 9,000 today. They have come to the city because of the availability of jobs and a welcoming attitude toward them.

Many Nebraskans' ancestors arrived as European immigrants in the 1800s. They hoped to start new lives as pioneer farmers. People of German heritage make up the largest ancestry group in Nebraska. German Americans are concentrated in the eastern part of the state. The next-largest groups are Irish, English, Swedish, and Czech. Among all the states, Nebraska is home to the largest percentage of Czech Americans.

Where Nebraskans Live

FAQ

Q8 WHERE ARE NEBRASKA'S NATIVE AMERICAN RESERVATIONS?

A8 The Omaha and Winnebago reservations occupy all of Thurston County, in eastern Nebraska. The Santee Sioux reservation is in northeastern Nebraska, near Niobrara. It used to be a Ponca reservation. Poncas, also centered in Niobrara, are trying to regain their original lands.

The colors on this map indicate population density throughout the state. The darker the color, the more people live there.

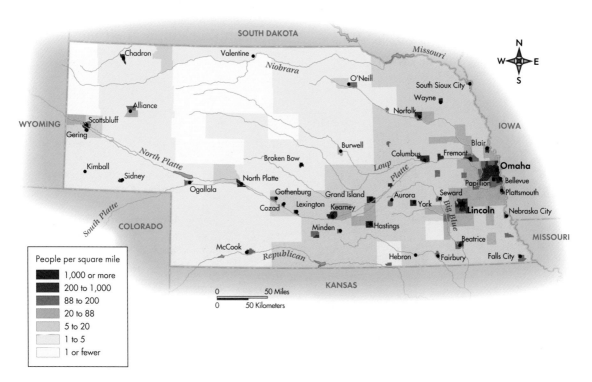

72

MINI-BIO

REUBEN SNAKE: YOUR HUMBLE SERPENT

Reuben Snake (1937–1993) had a sense of humor about his name. He sometimes called himself "Your Humble Serpent." But as an activist for Native American rights, he was dead serious. He campaigned tirelessly to protect Native lands, preserve Native culture, and improve education and health care for his people. Snake served as chairman of the American Indian Movement (AIM). As chairman of Nebraska's Winnebago tribe, he turned the reservation into a thriving economic community. Snake served on many national committees for Indian rights. He also worked with indigenous people's groups in other countries.

? Want to know more? Visit www.factsfornow.scholastic.com and enter the keyword **Nebraska**.

Four hundred years ago, Nebraska was solely the domain of Native Americans. Over the years, tens of thousands were killed, wiped out by diseases, or removed to other states. Those who remained were confined to reservations. Today, roughly 24,000 American Indians and Alaskan Natives live in Nebraska.

CELEBRATING TRADITIONS

Nebraska's many ethnic groups celebrate their heritage with annual festivals. They're lively celebrations, with traditional costumes, music, and foods. Every August, Czech Americans hold the Czech Festival in Wilber. Both Oakland and Stromsburg celebrate Swedish festivals in June. Omaha holds an Italian festival in July. Mexican Americans in Scottsbluff celebrate their heritage with

People QuickFacts

Source: U.S. Census Bureau, 2010 census

White persons: 82.1%

Hispanic or Latino persons: 9.2%

Black or African American persons: 4.4%

Asian persons: 1.7%

People of two or more races: 1.6%

American Indian and Alaska Native persons: 0.8%

Native Hawaiian and Other Pacific Islander: 0.1%

People of some other race: 0.1%

Nebraska Population Growth

This chart shows Nebraska's population growth between 1860 and 2010.

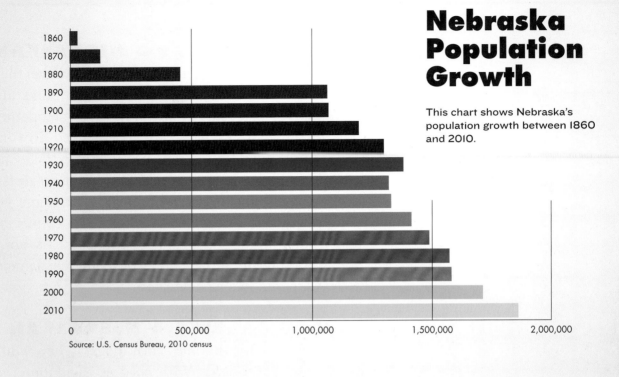

Source: U.S. Census Bureau, 2010 census

Cinco de Mayo (May 5). Native Americans come from miles around to attend powwows on Nebraska's Indian reservations.

Frontiersman Buffalo Bill Cody publicly debuted his Wild West Show in Omaha in 1883. It featured spectacular feats of horseback riding, shooting, roping, and other skills. Cody was outspoken about women's rights and Native American rights, and his performers included both women and Indians. Today, the town's Nebraskaland Days festival includes the Buffalo Bill Rodeo.

Many other rodeos are held throughout the state. They include Nebraska's Big Rodeo in Burwell and the Rodeo and Stock Show in Omaha. Creative cowboys and cowgirls meet in Valentine every October. They share their experiences through poems and songs at the Cowboy Poetry Gathering.

HOW TO TALK LIKE A NEBRASKAN

Like people in other states, Nebraskans have their own special choice of words for common items and situations. A dialect survey begun in 1999 documented some of those preferences. For food picked up from a restaurant, most Nebraskans use the term "take-out" instead of "carry-out." The end of a loaf of bread is a "heel" rather than a "crust." Store-bought items are brought home in a "bag" not a "sack." Soft drinks are "pop" rather than "soda." A long sandwich is not a "hero" or a "hoagie" but a "sub." These are just some of the ways to talk like a Nebraskan.

HOW TO EAT LIKE A NEBRASKAN

Do you like popcorn and corn dogs? Then you'd love living in Nebraska. With corn as their top crop, Nebraskans find lots of ways to eat it. They munch on corn bread, corn muffins, corn dogs, popcorn, corn-flakes, corn chowder, and plain old corn on the cob. Beef cattle eat that corn, too, and steaks and other beef products are also popular foods.

Nebraska's Czech community contributes a lot to local cuisine. Czech specialties include duck, potato dumplings, sauerkraut, sausages, and pastries called kolaches. For the Czech Festival in Wilber, cooks prepare close to 250,000 kolaches!

Corn on the cob is one of the special treats of summer!

MENU

WHAT'S ON THE MENU IN NEBRASKA?

★ ★ ★

Milk

Reuben sandwiches

It's said that Omaha grocer Reuben Kulakofsky invented the Reuben sandwich. One night in 1925, some men were playing poker in Omaha's Blackstone Hotel. They got hungry, and the grocer was asked to send over some food. He threw together some sandwiches of corned beef, Swiss cheese, and sauerkraut on rye bread. The sandwich was so popular that the owner put it on the hotel menu and named it after the grocer.

Eskimo Pies

Christian Nelson invented these ice cream sandwiches. He called them I-Scream Bars. But he couldn't get any company to manufacture them. So he took his idea to candy maker Russell Stover in Omaha. Stover changed the sandwich's name to Eskimo Pie.

State drinks

Nebraska got two tasty new state symbols in 1998. Milk was declared Nebraska's official state beverage, and Kool-Aid (invented in 1927 by Edwin Perkins in Hastings, Nebraska) became the official state soft drink.

Popcorn

Who doesn't like a warm handful of freshly made popcorn? Nebraska is an important producer of this tasty treat. Just go easy on the salt and butter!

TRY THIS RECIPE
Nebraska Corn Bread

What's a better food to represent the Cornhusker State than corn bread? Hot tip: You can use this same recipe to make corn muffins or corn dogs! (Be sure to have an adult nearby to help.)

Ingredients:
Makes 16 servings
1 cup flour
¼ cup sugar
½ teaspoon salt
3 teaspoons baking powder
1 cup yellow cornmeal
¼ cup shortening
1 cup milk
1 egg, lightly beaten

Instructions:
Preheat the oven to 425°F. Mix the flour, sugar, salt, and baking powder together and sift it twice. Stir in the cornmeal. In a separate bowl, mix the shortening, milk, and egg till blended. Stir in the dry ingredients and beat for about 1 minute. Pour the mixture into a greased 8-inch-square baking pan. Bake for 20 to 25 minutes. Cool on a rack. Cut into 2-inch squares.

Corn bread

WILLA CATHER: HOMETOWN TALES

As she was growing up in Red Cloud, Willa Cather (1873–1947) kept her eyes and ears open. Many of the stories she wrote as an adult take place in Red Cloud, and many of her characters are based on people she knew there. Cather published 12 novels, as well as many poems and short stories. Her novel *My Ántonia* is the story of a Czech immigrant girl's hardships and successes. *O Pioneers!* and *Death Comes for the Archbishop* are also American classics. Cather received the 1923 Pulitzer Prize for her novel *One of Ours*, about a pioneer's grandson who goes off to fight in World War I. Cather's childhood home in Red Cloud is a Nebraska state historic site.

Want to know more? Visit www.factsfornow .scholastic.com and enter the keyword **Nebraska**.

NEBRASKA AUTHORS

Pioneers and Native Americans have inspired the work of many Nebraska writers. Pulitzer Prize-winner Willa Cather (1873–1947) of Red Cloud explored prairie life in her books. Her novels *O Pioneers!* and *My Ántonia* show the struggles of Nebraska's early pioneers. Mari Sandoz (1896–1966) wrote novels that describe the hardships of Nebraska homesteaders, such as her immigrant father, whom she memorialized in *Old Jules*. She also wrote about injustices against Native Americans in books such as *Crazy Horse: The Strange Man of the Oglala* and *The Battle of Little Big Horn*.

Pioneer life in the Midwest is a major theme in the stories of Bess Streeter Aldrich (1881–1954). Many of her stories are set in the town of Elmwood, where she lived. Her most famous novel, *A Lantern in Her Hand*, is a tribute to her mother and other pioneer women.

Dorothy Thomas (1898–1990) based many of her short stories on the lives of people she met as a schoolteacher in western Nebraska. Her short story collection *The Getaway and Other Stories* revolves around families she knew in Scottsbluff.

John G. Neihardt (1881–1973) wrote *A Cycle of the West*, a collection of five epic poems about U.S. settlement on the Great Plains and its disruption of Native American cultures. He also wrote down the personal

Nebraska author John G. Neihardt wrote about Native Americans and how the arrival of settlers affected them.

narratives of an Oglala Sioux holy man in *Black Elk Speaks*. He became Nebraska's poet lauriate in 1921.

Nebraska poet Ted Kooser (1939–) was named poet laureate of the United States (2004–2006). A poet receiving this honor is entrusted with raising people's awareness of poetry in everyday life.

ARTISTS AND CRAFTSPEOPLE

Many well-known artists have a Nebraska connection. Artist Robert Henri (1865–1929) was born Robert Henry Cozad. His father founded the town of Cozad, Nebraska, where Robert grew up. In the early 1900s, Henri founded the Ash Can school of art, which favored painting real-

FAMILY HISTORIES

Imagine hearing real-life tales about Daniel Boone, Abraham Lincoln, and other historical figures. That's what it was like for Wilma Pitchford Hays (1907–2006) as she was growing up. Her parents and her two grandmothers told her stories about her ancestors' experiences in the Revolutionary War, the Civil War, and other conflicts. As an adult, Hays wrote more than 45 children's books. She included many of those childhood tales in her own fiction books, such as *Abe Lincoln's Birthday* and *The Scarlet Badge*. Hays was born in Fullerton.

MINI-BIO

GERARDO MEZA: COMMUNITY MURALIST

When he was 10, Gerardo Meza (1963–) of Lincoln did his first painting. Today, he expresses his Mexican heritage in both paintings and giant, colorful murals, or wall paintings. His art reflects many Hispanic cultural themes, especially the importance of the family. One Meza mural covers a wall on the Lincoln Hispanic Center building. Another mural adorns a pedestrian tunnel in Lincoln. For both projects, Meza enlisted the help of children from the community.

 Want to know more? Visit www.factsfornow.scholastic.com and enter the keyword **Nebraska**.

SEE IT HERE!

PAINTING THE FRONTIER

Omaha's Joslyn Art Museum has more than 11,000 artworks related to the American West, as well as Europe, Asia, and ancient cultures. Among its collections are paintings by Swiss artist Karl Bodmer. On an 1832 trip up the Missouri River, he painted watercolors of Native Americans and frontier landscapes—considered some of the finest paintings of the American West.

istic pictures of poor people. Paul Swan (1883–1972) was a painter and sculptor, as well as a dancer. He made portraits and sculptures of some of the leading figures of his time, including presidents Franklin D. Roosevelt and John F. Kennedy, aviator Charles Lindbergh, and author Willa Cather. Aaron Pyle (1909–1972) lived in Chappell for most of his life. He is known for his vivid paintings of Western life and landscapes.

Angel DeCora (1871–1919), a Nebraska Winnebago, was a painter, illustrator, and designer.

Paul Swan working on a sculpture

She was best known for her book illustrations using Native American designs. Today, Nebraska's Native Americans continue many of their ancient craft traditions. They make baskets, blankets, pottery, jewelry, clothing, and other handcrafted items. Many Nebraska museums display Native American arts and crafts. They include the University of Nebraska State Museum, the Great Plains Art Museum, and the Museum of Nebraska History in Lincoln; the Joslyn Art Museum in Omaha; and the Angel DeCora Museum in Winnebago.

WINNEBAGO ARTIST

Angel DeCora (1871–1919) was born Hinook-Mahiwi-Kilinaka on the Winnebago reservation in Dakota County. She studied art at Smith College in Massachusetts, the Drexel Institute in Pennsylvania, and the Boston Museum of Fine Arts, becoming the first Winnebago woman to attend college. DeCora illustrated books and magazine articles, using her version of Native American designs. DeCora also toured the country speaking on Native American issues.

The interior courtyard at the Joslyn Art Museum

AARON DOUGLAS: FATHER OF AFRICAN AMERICAN ART

As an artist, Aaron Douglas (1899–1979) used African themes, subjects, and designs in his vibrant paintings. He's often called the father of African American Art. Born in Kansas, Douglas attended the University of Nebraska, where he received his bachelor of arts degree in 1922. In New York City, he joined the Harlem Renaissance movement of African American artists and writers. Later, he founded the Art Department at Fisk University in Nashville, Tennessee, and taught there for 29 years.

? Want to know more? Visit www.factsfornow.scholastic.com and enter the keyword **Nebraska**.

PERFORMING ARTS

When it comes to performing arts, Lincoln and Omaha take the lead. Nationally recognized music and dance groups perform in the Lied Center for Performing Arts at the University of Nebraska in Lincoln. The city is also proud of its Lincoln Community Playhouse, Lincoln Friends of Chamber Music, and Abendmusik: Lincoln. Omaha is home to the Omaha Symphony Orchestra, Opera Omaha, the Omaha Theater Company for Young People, and the Nebraska Wind Symphony. The Omaha Community Playhouse is the nation's largest community theater. It takes its shows on the road in the Nebraska Theatre Caravan touring company.

Many famous movie stars have come

Fans enjoy a rock concert at Sokol Auditorium in Omaha.

from Nebraska. They include Fred Astaire (1899–1987), an actor known for his smooth dance steps; Marlon Brando (1924–2004), who won an Academy Award for *The Godfather*; and Swoosie Kurtz (1944–), an award-winning stage actress. They left the state at an early age. Actor Henry Fonda (1905–1982) was born in Grand Island and grew up in Omaha. He started his acting career at the Omaha Community Playhouse. Fonda went on to star in *The Grapes of Wrath, 12 Angry Men,* and dozens of other films. In 1981, he won an Academy Award for his role in *On Golden Pond*.

EDUCATION

Missionaries opened Nebraska's first schools to teach Native American children about Christianity and European ways. Students were taken from their families and forbidden to speak their Native languages, and so they lost an important part of their ancient culture.

Nebraska's first school for white children was at the military post of Fort Atkinson. It opened in 1820. One-room schools were the rule during the days of early settlers. Kids attended school when they were not needed to work on their family's farm.

Today, children in Nebraska are required to attend school from ages 7 through 16. Many of Nebraska's school districts are in rural areas. In some places, kids still get their education in one-room schoolhouses!

MINI-BIO

HAROLD LLOYD: SILENT FILM STAR

Harold Lloyd (1893–1971) had early movie audiences rolling in the aisles with laughter as star of nearly 200 comedy films between 1917 and 1947. Many of his popular films were silent, and they often featured wacky, thrilling chase scenes and daredevil stunts. In the movie Safety Last! (1923), Lloyd actually hangs from the hands of a clock high above a city street. After his film career ended, he worked in radio as a director and program host and appeared as himself on several TV shows.

Want to know more? Visit www.factsfornow.scholastic.com and enter the keyword **Nebraska**.

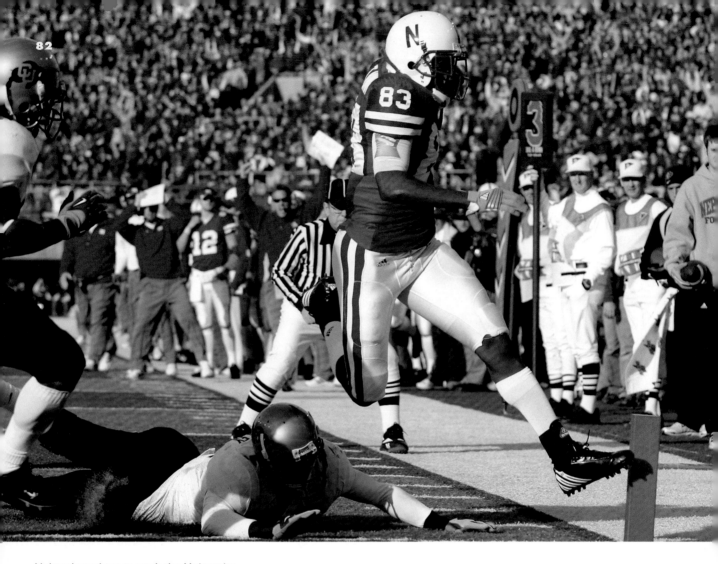

Nebraskans love to pack the University of Nebraska's Memorial Stadium on Saturdays in the fall to watch the Cornhuskers.

Nebraska's leading university is the University of Nebraska. The state's first legislature founded it in Lincoln in 1869. The university now has campuses in Lincoln, Omaha, and Kearney, as well as a medical center in Omaha. Scientists at the various campuses conduct research in a wide variety of fields. Creighton University is in Omaha. Founded in 1878, it's run by the Jesuit order of Catholic priests. Creighton is known for its outstanding schools of medicine, dentistry, and natural sciences. Nebraska also has more than a dozen other private colleges and universities, as well as state colleges and community colleges.

GO HUSKERS!

Round up all the football fans across the country. Then ask them what Nebraska means to them. They'll say the Cornhuskers! Cornhuskers, or just Huskers for short, are the sports teams at the University of Nebraska in Lincoln. The perennial power-house Cornhuskers football team has five national championships to its credit. The Huskers play their home games in the campus's Memorial Stadium.

Cornhuskers compete in a wide variety of men's and women's Division I sports and have won national championships in football, volleyball, bowling, track and field, and gymnastics.

Nebraska is a hot spot for college baseball. Omaha is the home of the College Baseball World Series. Five Nebraskans have been inducted into the Baseball Hall of Fame—Sam "Wahoo" Crawford, Grover Cleveland Alexander, Bob Gibson, Arthur "Dazzy" Vance, and Richie Ashburn. They're featured in the Museum of Nebraska Major League Baseball in St. Paul.

The U.S. Amateur Confederation of Roller Skating has its headquarters in Lincoln. It often holds its national championships there. Lincoln is home to the organization's museum. Nebraskans also like to go canoeing, bicycling, and hiking. Maybe because of their pioneer roots, they enjoy vigorous outdoor activities.

MINI-BIO

BOB GIBSON: HALL OF FAME PITCHER

During the 1960s and early 1970s, Bob Gibson (1935–) was the most feared pitcher in baseball. Born in Omaha, the hard-throwing righthander was a nine-time National League (NL) All-Star and a two-time NL Cy Young Award winner. In 1968, he hurled 13 shutouts and set a modern baseball record by posting a puny 1.12 earned run average. His amazing accomplishments that year earned him the league's Most Valuable Player award. Gibson was inducted into the Baseball Hall of Fame in 1981.

? Want to know more? Visit www.factsfornow.scholastic.com and enter the keyword **Nebraska**.

READ ABOUT

The lobby of the Nebraska state capitol

GOVERNMENT

★

O NE DAY IN 1974, STUDENTS AT CAL-VERT ELEMENTARY SCHOOL IN AUBURN WERE READING A CLASS-ROOM MAGAZINE. It said the honeybee was the state insect in only one state. The kids discussed honeybees and how important they are to Nebraska. In their opinion, the honeybee should be Nebraska's state insect, too. So they wrote letters to their state lawmakers and made it happen. The honeybee measure was signed into law in 1975.

Representing Nebraska

This list shows the number of elected officials who represent Nebraska, both on the state and national levels.

OFFICE	NUMBER	LENGTH OF TERM
State senators	49	4 years
U.S. senators	2	6 years
U.S. representatives	3	2 years
Presidential electors	5	—

THE CENTER OF GOVERNMENT

Those students in Auburn understood how their state government worked and how new laws were made. That's how they were able to turn their vision into law. They knew that their state lawmakers—along with other important government officials—met in the state capitol. That's the main government building in Lincoln, Nebraska's capital city. Governing power in Nebraska is divided into three branches—the legislative, executive, and judicial. Each branch has a special job to do.

The roles of the various government branches are outlined in the state constitution. This document defines how the state government works. Nebraska

Nebraska state capitol in Lincoln

Capital City

This map shows places of interest in Lincoln, Nebraska's capital city.

Capitol Facts

Here are some fascinating facts about Nebraska's state capitol.

Exterior height: . . . . . 000 feet (121 m)
Height of statue on top: . .19 feet (5.8 m)
Number of floors: 22
Width of base: . . . . 437 feet (133 m)
Location: . . . . . .15th and K Streets, Lincoln
Construction dates: 1922–1932
Cost of construction: . . . .$9.8 million

adopted its first constitution in 1866, before statehood. A new constitution was drawn up in 1875. Since then, many amendments, or changes, have been added to the constitution. An amendment may be proposed by the legislature, the people, or a constitutional convention. An amendment becomes a law if it is approved by three-fifths of the legislature and a majority of the state's voters.

THE LEGISLATIVE BRANCH

How many houses are in the U.S. Congress? Two. How many houses are in 49 of the 50 state legislatures? Two. And how many houses are in Nebraska's state legislature? One!

Q8 HOW MANY STATE CAPITOLS ARE SKYSCRAPERS?

A8 Only four states have skyscraper capitols—Florida, Louisiana, Nebraska, and North Dakota.

Keystone XL Pipeline

THINK ABOUT IT!

Pro:

The proposed Keystone XL Pipeline would carry oil-soaked clay and soil 1,661 miles (2,673 km) from Canada to oil refineries on the Gulf Coast of Texas. The pipeline would run through several states, including Nebraska. Supporters of the pipeline say that it would create hundreds of construction jobs. It would also lessen America's dependence on foreign oil in order to meet the country's energy needs. "Energy independence is tied to national security, and being independent makes us safer," said U.S. senator John Hoeven of North Dakota.

Con:

In 2011, Nebraska legislators voted to have the pipeline rerouted away from Nebraska's Ogallala Aquifer, a major water source, and other environmentally sensitive areas in the region. Many Nebraskans fear that an oil spill would seriously harm these areas. In 2012, President Barack Obama rejected plans to run the pipeline through these regions. New routes were proposed and approved by Governor Dave Heineman in 2013, but the debate over whether the pipeline should run through Nebraska at all continues.

Sources: *New York Times*, April 18, 2013; *Businessweek*, September 16, 2013.

FAQ

Q8 DID NEBRASKA INVENT THE UNICAMERAL LEGISLATURE?

A8 Not exactly. Most of the 13 colonies had unicameral legislatures. When they became states, they all switched to two-house legislatures except three—Georgia, Pennsylvania, and Vermont. Those three eventually adopted bicameral legislatures in 1789, 1790, and 1836, respectively.

The nation and each of the states have legislatures. Their job is to make laws. Except for Nebraska, these legislatures are all bicameral. That is, they all have two chambers, or houses. In most cases, those two houses are a senate and a house of representatives. But Nebraska is different. It has a unicameral, or one-house, legislature. All of its 49 members are called senators.

In other legislatures, most candidates run for election as members of either the Democratic Party or the Republican Party. These races are called primary elections, or primaries for short. Then the winning Democrat and the top Republican face each other in the general election. But not in Nebraska. In senate primaries, a candidate's political party is not even listed on the **ballot**. The two candidates who get the most votes run against each other.

THE EXECUTIVE BRANCH

The job of the executive branch of government is to carry out the laws. Nebraska's governor heads the executive branch. He or she is elected to a four-year term. Other elected officials in the executive branch are the lieutenant governor, the secretary of state, the treasurer, and the auditor. Voters also elect members of the state board of education, the board of regents of the University of Nebraska, and the public utilities commission.

The executive branch also includes several departments that oversee important state matters. These include the departments of environmental quality, motor vehicles, labor, and roads.

THE JUDICIAL BRANCH

The judicial branch consists of judges who preside over courts. The job of this branch is to apply the laws. That is, the judges examine the laws to decide whether someone has broken them.

WORD TO KNOW

ballot *a sheet of paper on which people mark their voting choices (some places conduct voting with electronic machines rather than by paper ballots).*

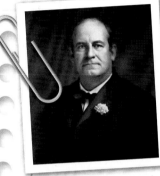

MINI-BIO

WILLIAM JENNINGS BRYAN: THE GREAT COMMONER

William Jennings Bryan (1860–1925) was Nebraska's first Democratic congressman. He served as U.S. secretary of state under President Woodrow Wilson (1913–1915). A powerful public speaker, Bryan was well known for supporting the rights of common, working-class people, and his nickname was the Great Commoner. He once said, "My place in history will depend on what I can do for the people and not on what the people can do for me." Bryan ran for president in 1896, 1900, and 1908, but he never won. A deeply religious man, Bryan fought against teaching evolution and legalizing alcoholic beverages until his death in 1925. Fairview, his family home in Lincoln, is open to the public.

Want to know more? Visit www.factsfornow.scholastic.com and enter the keyword **Nebraska**.

Nebraska's State Government

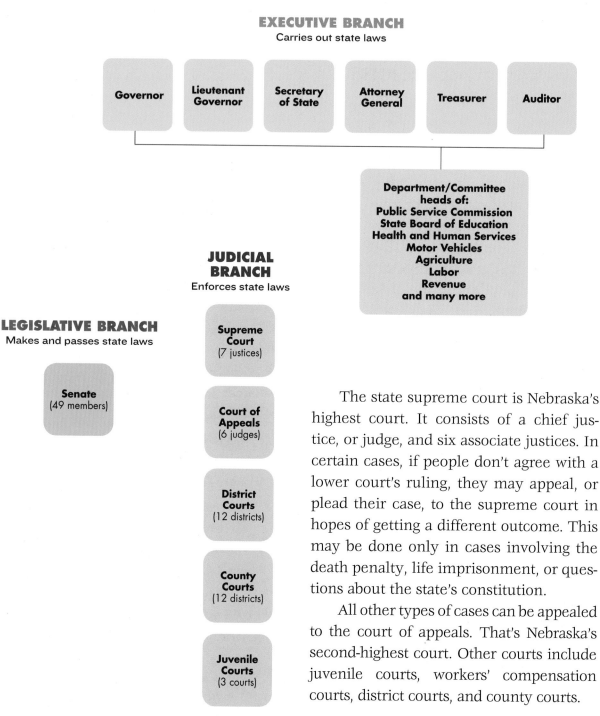

EXECUTIVE BRANCH
Carries out state laws

| Governor | Lieutenant Governor | Secretary of State | Attorney General | Treasurer | Auditor |

Department/Committee heads of:
Public Service Commission
State Board of Education
Health and Human Services
Motor Vehicles
Agriculture
Labor
Revenue
and many more

JUDICIAL BRANCH
Enforces state laws

LEGISLATIVE BRANCH
Makes and passes state laws

Senate
(49 members)

Supreme Court
(7 justices)

Court of Appeals
(6 judges)

District Courts
(12 districts)

County Courts
(12 districts)

Juvenile Courts
(3 courts)

The state supreme court is Nebraska's highest court. It consists of a chief justice, or judge, and six associate justices. In certain cases, if people don't agree with a lower court's ruling, they may appeal, or plead their case, to the supreme court in hopes of getting a different outcome. This may be done only in cases involving the death penalty, life imprisonment, or questions about the state's constitution.

All other types of cases can be appealed to the court of appeals. That's Nebraska's second-highest court. Other courts include juvenile courts, workers' compensation courts, district courts, and county courts.

LOCAL GOVERNMENT

Nebraska has 93 counties. Voters in each county elect a clerk, a sheriff, a treasurer, an attorney, a superintendent of schools, and a surveyor, who measures land and establishes property lines. Counties with a large population also elect an assessor, who places a value on property so it can be taxed appropriately; a clerk of the district court; and a registrar of deeds, who maintains records related to land sales.

MINI-BIO

JEAN STOTHERT: MAYOR OF OMAHA

In 2012, Jean Stothert (1954–) became the first woman to be elected mayor in Omaha, winning 57 percent of the vote. If elected, she promised to cut her mayor's salary by 10 percent and give the money to the city. She also pledged not to use taxpayer money to rent an automobile or pay for gasoline, as previous officeholders had. Born in Illinois, Stothert began her professional career as a nurse. In 1992, she moved with her family to Omaha and started her career in public service on a local board of education.

? **Want to know more?** Visit www.factsfornow.scholastic.com and enter the keyword **Nebraska**.

In 1986, Nebraska became the first state where two women—Kay A. Orr and Helen Boosalis—ran against each other for governor. Orr won, becoming the nation's first female Republican governor.

MINI-BIO

PATSY TAKEMOTO MINK: FIGHTING FOR EQUALITY

When Patsy Takemoto Mink (1927–2002) was a student at the University of Nebraska (1946–1947), Asians and people of color had to live in separate dormitories from the white students. Mink organized students and community leaders in protest of this segregation policy. She succeeded in ending it. Born in Hawaii, Mink went on to represent Hawaii in the U.S. House of Representatives for 12 terms (1965–1977 and 1990–2002). She was the first nonwhite woman ever elected to Congress.

? Want to know more? Visit www.factsfornow .scholastic.com and enter the keyword **Nebraska**.

Within each county are cities, villages, and townships. Large cities, such as Omaha and Lincoln, are governed by a mayor and city council. Some cities elect a city manager instead. In villages, the citizens elect a board of trustees.

Nebraskans can vote for the government officials they want. But they have other ways to

Nebraska Counties

This map shows the 93 counties in Nebraska. Lincoln, the state capital, is indicated with a star.

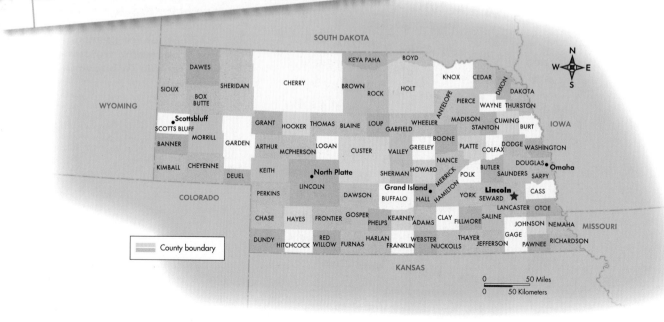

make their voices heard. One is the initiative. It allows the citizens themselves to initiate, or propose, a law they want passed or changed. After a vote, the law goes to the legislature for approval. A 1966 initiative, for example, prohibits the state from charging property taxes. Another tool is the referendum. That's a way for voters to join forces and repeal, or cancel, a law the legislature has passed. In 2006, voters used a referendum to repeal a law that reorganized school districts.

Justices on the Nebraska Supreme Court, the highest court in the state, listen to arguments in a case.

NEBRASKA POLITICIANS IN THE SPOTLIGHT

- Deb Fischer (1951–) became the first woman from Nebraska to be elected to the U.S. Senate, in 2012.
- Gerald Ford (1913–2006) was the 38th president of the United States, holding office from 1974 to 1977.
- Chuck Hagel (1946–) took office as a U.S. senator in 1997 and served until 2009. In 2013, President Barack Obama appointed him the U.S. secretary of defense.
- Mike Johanns (1950–) was the mayor of Lincoln (1991–1998) and governor of Nebraska (1999–2005). He served as U.S. secretary of agriculture from 2005 to 2007.
- Bob Kerrey (1943–) served as Nebraska's governor (1983–1987) and a U.S. senator (1989–2001). In 1992, he ran unsuccessfully for the Democratic presidential nomination.

State Flag

Nebraska's state flag features an image of the state seal in silver and gold. It is displayed on a field of blue. In 1925, Nebraska adopted a state banner with this design. But it was not until 1963 that the design became Nebraska's official state flag.

State Seal

Nebraska's state seal is a circle containing symbols of the state's history and economy. In the center is a blacksmith with hammer and anvil. He represents the mechanical arts. A settler's cabin and sheaves of wheat represent Nebraska's agriculture. In the background is a steamboat on the Missouri River. Behind that, a train heads toward the Rocky Mountains.

At the top of the seal is a banner with the state motto, "Equality before the law." The circle is surrounded with the words "Great Seal of the State of Nebraska, March 1st, 1867." That's the date when Nebraska became a state.

READ ABOUT

Trains crisscross
Nebraska carrying
goods to all
sections of the
United States.

CHAPTER EIGHT

ECONOMY

★

EXPLORER STEPHEN LONG WASN'T VERY IMPRESSED WITH NEBRASKA IN THE 1800s. He said it was "almost wholly unfit for cultivation." He should see Nebraska now! It's one of the nation's top farming states. Drive through Nebraska, and you'll see mile after mile of rolling farmland and pastures. The state exports its farm products to countries all over the world. Nebraskans produce much more than farm products, though. The state is a major center for insurance, finance, food processing, railroad transportation, and many other industries.

SERVICE INDUSTRIES

Agriculture was once Nebraska's major industry. Then the manufacturing industry surpassed farming. Today, service industries bring the most money into Nebraska's economy. People in the service industries provide all kinds of helpful services. They include nurses, teachers, lawyers, repair technicians, computer operators, hairdressers, truck drivers, grocery store employees, and bankers.

Omaha is the center for the state's financial services. It's the headquarters for Mutual of Omaha, a large health insurance company. Omaha native and billionaire Warren Buffett founded Berkshire Hathaway, which owns many insurance companies and is based in his hometown. Omaha is the home of the Gallup Organization, too. It conducts surveys to find out people's opinions on a variety of issues.

The wholesale trade is another service industry. Wholesalers sell goods to companies rather than directly to consumers. Omaha's ConAgra Foods is one of the nation's biggest wholesale food companies. It sells foods to supermarkets and restaurants. Much of that food is shipped out on the Omaha-based Union Pacific Railroad. It's the country's largest railroad.

Nebraska's government services include public schools and military bases. Offutt Air Force Base, near Bellevue, houses the U.S. Strategic Command (USSTRATCOM). It's in charge of the country's nuclear weapons forces.

MINI-BIO

WARREN BUFFETT: BILLIONS AND BILLIONS AND BILLIONS . . .

What would you do if you had billions of dollars? If you were Warren Buffett (1930–), you'd give it away. Buffett is one of the richest people in the world. In 2006, Buffett decided to give most of his fortune—$37 billion!—to charity. Born in Omaha, Buffett still lives there. He founded Berkshire Hathaway, an Omaha-based investment company. Unless he's traveling, Buffett doesn't carry a cell phone!

❓ Want to know more? Visit www.factsfornow.scholastic.com and enter the keyword Nebraska.

One of Nebraska's most important industries is food processing. Here a group of volunteer testers are trying new food products.

Strangely enough, military operations led to Nebraska's modern telecommunications industry. USSTRATCOM used to be the Strategic Air Command (SAC). In the 1960s, SAC installed a top-notch communications system in the Omaha area. In the 1980s, private businesses began using that system, too. As a result, Omaha became a world leader in selling things through phone calls, or telemarketing. Omaha also developed a huge toll-free calling industry. The city is sometimes called the "1-800 Capital of the World."

MANUFACTURING INDUSTRIES

Can you guess what Nebraska's leading factory goods are? If you guessed food products, you're right! Naturally, the state's leading food products involve meat and grains. Nebraska is a leading center for meatpacking. Butchers at meat plants cut up beef and pork and package it for sale. Truckers haul corn, wheat, and other crops to food plants. Workers at these plants make cattle feed, breakfast cereals, baked goods, canned and frozen vegetables, and many other foods.

Chemicals are next in manufacturing importance. Nebraska's chemical plants make medicines, bug killers, fertilizers, and other products. Machines are the next-ranking factory goods, and farm equipment is the major type of machinery. That includes tractors, harvesters, and irrigation equipment.

Some of Nebraska's other factory goods are medical instruments, motor vehicles, electrical equipment, and plastics.

AGRICULTURE

Nebraska is sometimes called the nation's breadbasket. That's because the state provides so much of the country's grain. Farms and ranches cover about 93 percent of Nebraska.

Nebraska's nickname is the Cornhusker State, because corn is Nebraska's leading crop. In fact, Nebraska is the nation's number-three corn producer, after Iowa and Illinois. And what about the "husker" part? Husking means removing the leafy husks from the ears of corn.

Cattle, hogs, and other livestock are the state's most valuable farm products. They account for about half of Nebraska's farm income. Beef cattle are the leading farm animals. About one-fourth of Nebraska's corn ends up as food for livestock. More than 38 percent of the corn is made into ethanol fuel and other industrial products. And another 25 percent of the corn is exported to other states and to foreign countries.

Other valuable crops in Nebraska are soybeans, winter wheat, and hay. Corn and wheat grow throughout much

SEE IT HERE!

THE DAILY GRIND

How does Nebraska's wheat turn into flour? Today, food plants use big, electric-powered machines to grind the wheat grains into powdery flour. But in the 1800s, the grinding was done at flour mills that got their power from river water turning a giant wheel. You can see how it was done at the Neligh Mill State Historic Site in Neligh. Mills like this were some of Nebraska's earliest factories. They helped build the state's food-processing industry.

Top Products

Agriculture Cattle and calves, corn, hogs, wheat

Manufacturing Food products, chemicals, medical equipment, machinery

Mining Petroleum, sand and gravel

NEBRASKA INVENTORS

Invention	Inventor	Date	Location
Hallmark cards	Joyce Hall	1908	Norfolk
Vise-Grip pliers	William Petersen	1924	DeWitt
Kool-Aid	Edwin Perkins	1927	Hastings
Strobe light	Harold Edgerton	1931	Fremont (birthplace)
CliffsNotes study guides	Clifton Hillegass	1958	Rising City (birthplace)

Major Agricultural and Mining Products

This map shows where Nebraska's major agricultural and mining products come from. See a chicken? That means poultry products are found there.

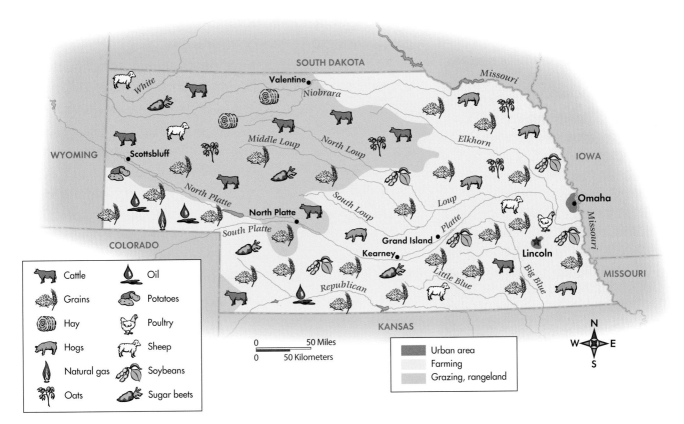

Corn is Nebraska's leading crop. Here, a farmer harvests corn.

CROP CIRCLES

Fly over Nebraska, and you'll see big green circles in the middle of crop fields. They're not made by aliens from outer space. They're made by center pivot irrigation! How does this system work? A long, thin water pipeline sweeps around in a circle, just like a clock's hand. As the pipeline swings round and round, it sprinkles water on the field. This process makes the crops grow in a circular pattern. Nebraska uses center pivot irrigation more than any other state. It's also the top manufacturer of this type of irrigation equipment.

of the state. Most soybeans are raised in the eastern half of Nebraska. Much of the state's hay crop grows in the Sand Hills region. Sugar beets, pinto beans, and other dry beans grow in the irrigated fields of western Nebraska. More than one-third of Nebraska's farmland uses irrigation. This protects the farming industry against drought.

Nebraska farmers have faced some tough challenges in recent years. The summer drought of 2012 in Nebraska and other Great Plains states drove the price of corn to a record level of $8.20 per bushel. The price of soybeans, Nebraska's second-most-important cash crop, also soared to a record level, more than $17.30 per bushel. From 2011 to 2012, the price of farmland in Nebraska jumped 31 percent. That's the highest annual increase in the 34 years that records for land sales have been kept. The demand for prime land remains high among wealthy farmers and investors. However, high prices discourage smaller farmers from buying and expanding their businesses.

MINING

Mining is a rather small industry in Nebraska. It accounts for less than half of 1 percent of the state's total income. Oil is the most valuable mining product. It's found in parts of western Nebraska.

Other mining products include sand and gravel, crushed stone, and clay. The sand and gravel have many uses, such as making concrete and controlling snow and ice on roadways. Crushed limestone is used in making cement and building roads. Clay is good for making bricks and pottery.

FAQ

Q8 HOW DO NEBRASKA'S FARM PRODUCTS RANK AMONG OTHER STATES?

A8 In 2012, Nebraska was one of the nation's top seven producers of cattle and calves, corn, soybeans, great northern beans, pinto beans, hogs, and pigs!

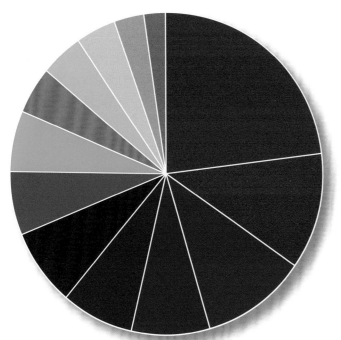

What Do Nebraskans Do?

This color-coded chart shows what industries Nebraskans work in.

23.3% Educational services, and health care and social assistance, 219,766

11.6% Retail trade, 109,589

10.7% Manufacturing, 100,964

8.1% Professional, scientific, and management, and administrative and waste management services, 76,624

7.6% Finance and insurance, and real estate and rental and leasing, 72,000

7.6% Arts, entertainment, and recreation, and accommodation and food services, 71,955

6.5% Construction, 60,891

6.0% Transportation and warehousing, and utilities, 56,606

4.8% Agriculture, forestry, fishing and hunting, and mining, 44,734

4.5% Other services, except public administration, 42,361

4.1% Public administration, 38,319

3.0% Wholesale trade, 27,894

2.1% Information, 19,567

Source: U.S. Census Bureau, 2010 census

CHAPTER NINE

TRAVEL GUIDE

TRAVEL GUIDE

★

FOLLOW THE PIONEER TRAILS, WATCH MIGRATING BIRDS, SEE SOME AWESOME FOSSILS, OR ENJOY NATIVE AMERICAN FESTIVALS. Watch a Wild West show, explore woods and Badlands, hunker in a sod house, or stroll through an indoor rain forest. Do these activities appeal to your sense of adventure? Then Nebraska's the place for you! Let's take a tour through this amazing land.

← Follow along with this travel map. We'll begin in Niobrara and travel all the way up to Harrison!

LEWIS AND CLARK TERRITORY

THINGS TO DO: Visit a Lewis and Clark campsite, enjoy Native American dances and foods, or see 10-million-year-old fossils that were buried in ash!

Niobrara

★ **Lewis and Clark Campsite:** See where the two explorers camped as they followed the Missouri River.

★ **Northern Ponca Powwow:** Visit in August to see costumed dancers perform their traditional dances.

Yankton

★ **Riverwalk:** Enjoy an exhibition of outdoor sculpture while walking along the scenic and historic Missouri River.

Macy

★ **Omaha Powwow:** Held on the weekend closest to August's full moon, this festival is a traditional harvest celebration.

Royal

★ **Ashfall Fossil Beds State Historical Park:** More than 10 million years ago, ash buried the animals here. They've been left in place right where they died, and you can see their remains at the Rhino Barn.

Rhino skeleton fossil

Winnebago

★ **Angel DeCora Memorial Museum/Research Center:** At this museum, you'll learn about Winnebago culture through clothing, baskets, and other traditional items. The museum is named after the first Winnebago woman to attend college.

★ **Winnebago Powwow:** Every July, Winnebago people from all over the country gather here to sing, dance, perform traditional ceremonies, and honor Chief Little Priest.

Walthill

★ **Susan LaFlesche Picotte Center:** Picotte, the nation's first Native American woman to earn a medical degree, originally built this site as a hospital for Native Americans. Now it's a national historic site.

FROM OMAHA TO LINCOLN

THINGS TO DO: Zoom up to the top of the skyscraper capitol, see a gigantic mammoth fossil, get face-to-face with wild animals, or see the world's largest ball of stamps!

Omaha

★ **Riverwalk:** Stroll along this walkway by the Missouri River and imagine the time when this area was a meeting place and trade center for 18th-century Native Americans, explorers, traders, and pioneers. Look toward the 21st-century city, and you'll see skyscrapers where many large corporations have their headquarters.

★ **Durham Museum:** Located in a restored 1930s railroad station, this museum features artifacts and multimedia presentations that depict the region's history.

★ **Henry Doorly Zoo:** Have a close encounter with wildlife at this gigantic zoo. Its Lied Jungle is the world's largest indoor rain forest. The zoo also features animals in a swamp, a desert, and an aquarium, as well as a petting zoo.

Henry Doorly Zoo

★ **Leon Myers Stamp Center:** Here you'll see the world's largest ball of stamps. It weighs 600 pounds (270 kilograms) and is made of 4,655,000 postage stamps!

Bellevue

★ **Sarpy County Museum:** Trace the region's history from prehistoric times to the present. You'll see displays on Native Americans, missionaries, early farmers, and Fort Crook, which is now Offutt Air Force Base. You'll also learn about the fur traders who founded Bellevue, Nebraska's oldest town, in 1823.

★ **National Children's Lewis and Clark Interpretive Art Wall:** That's a big name for an even bigger piece of art. It's 65 feet (20 m) long and 8 feet (2.4 m) high! Schoolkids from communities all along the explorers' route did the artwork on more than 700 handmade tiles. Each section tells the story of their journey in that region.

Lincoln

★ **State Capitol:** Take an elevator to the top floor for a great bird's-eye view of the city.

★ **Museum of Nebraska History:** Here you'll learn all about the people and events that shaped Nebraska throughout history.

★ **National Museum of Roller Skating:** Are you a roller skater or a Rollerblader? Check out this museum to learn more than you can imagine about skates, skaters, and skating.

★ **Lincoln Children's Zoo:** Get a kid's-eye view of leopards, crocodiles, camels, reindeer, and more. You can also ride a train around the grounds, see a harbor seal show, and watch butterflies emerge from their cocoons.

★ **International Quilt Study Center & Museum:** If you have parents or grandparents who make quilts, this museum is for you. See more than 3,500 quilts from more than 25 countries. The museum opened in its new building in 2008.

★ **University of Nebraska State Museum:** Gaze at the largest mammoth fossil ever found, on display at one of the nation's top fossil museums. Scientists dug it up near Wellfleet. Also on campus are Mueller Planetarium, Sheldon Memorial Art Gallery, and Lied Center for the Performing Arts.

SEE IT HERE!

THE TOWER OF THE PLAINS

Most state capitols are a few stories high, with a big dome on top. But Nebraska's capitol is a skyscraper. In downtown Lincoln, the state capitol is hard to miss. By law, no other structure in town may be higher than the capitol. This 22-story building is nicknamed the Tower of the Plains. It's topped by a golden dome, with a statue called the *Sower* on top. This statue of a farmer sowing grain stands for Nebraska's agriculture. Inside the capitol, you'll see wall paintings depicting Nebraska's Native American cultures and pioneer history.

FAQ

Q: HOW BIG IS THE MAMMOTH FOSSIL AT THE UNIVERSITY OF NEBRASKA STATE MUSEUM?

A: This giant beast measures more than 13 feet (4 m) tall at the shoulder.

PIONEER COUNTRY

THINGS TO DO: Nestle in a treetop tree house, see life-sized models of Lewis and Clark's boats, conduct your own science experiments, or sit in the world's largest porch swing!

Nebraska City

★ **Arbor Day Farm:** This 260-acre (105-ha) site used to belong to tree lover J. Sterling Morton, who founded Arbor Day. Go on the Tree Adventure, and you'll meet lots of wildlife along the forest trails. Or climb up to a tree house way up in the treetops, five stories above the ground!

★ **Missouri River Basin Lewis and Clark Interpretive Trail and Visitors Center:** Here you can explore life-sized replicas of the explorers' boats. You can also learn about some of the more than 300 plant and animal species that the explorers were the first to write about.

★ **Kregel Windmill Museum:** See the "workhorses" that pumped water and helped make farming in Nebraska possible. The museum opened in 2013 and is the last existing historic windmill factory.

Beatrice

★ **Homestead National Monument of America:** "Free land!" That's what drew settlers to the plains. This park and heritage center honors the pioneers who staked out new homes thanks to the Homestead Act and their own hard work. Check out the interactive exhibits, then explore historic structures along the trails. Here you'll see the home site of Daniel Freeman, the first homesteader.

Homestead National Monument of America

Hebron

★ **World's largest porch swing, located in Roosevelt Park:** Hop on—and bring your whole family and all your friends with you. This swing can seat 18 adults or 24 children!

Aurora

★ **Edgerton Explorit Center:** This is a great place to try some exciting, hands-on science experiments. For example, you can go snowboarding down a mountain in a virtual reality game or freeze your shadow on a wall. The museum is named for the Nebraska scientist who invented strobe lights.

PRAIRIE LAKES REGION

THINGS TO DO: Get a taste of pioneer life, watch sandhill cranes do their dance, see herds of wild horses and burros, or take in a rodeo!

Hastings

★ **Hastings Museum of Natural and Cultural History:** Explore lifelike displays showing many forms of animal life in their natural habitats, from polar bears to hummingbirds. See everyday gadgets that people used in the 1800s. Watch a film on the five-story IMAX screen. Or see a sky show in the planetarium!

Grand Island

★ **Nebraska State Fair:** If you're in the area in late August or early September, you can enjoy this exhibition of farm products, food, and entertainment.

The Nebraska State Fair

★ **Stuhr Museum of the Prairie Pioneer:** Immerse yourself in pioneer life at this living history museum.

Grand Island/Hastings/Kearney

★ **Sandhill crane migration:** You can see these magnificent birds in March and April along this stretch of the Platte River.

Minden

★ **Pioneer Village:** Among its attractions, from the 1800s and early 1900s, are a frontier fort, a real Pony Express station, a sod house, a toy store, and antiquecars, tractors, and flying machines.

Great Platte River Road Archway Monument

Kearney

★ **Great Platte River Road Archway Monument:** Pioneer life becomes an interactive adventure here. You'll witness buffalo stampedes, railroad construction, covered wagon travel, and much more.

Elm Creek

★ **Nebraska Wild Horse and Burro Facility:** Would you like to have a special kind of pet? Hundreds of wild horses and burros roam here, waiting for people to adopt them.

Gothenburg

★ **Sod House Museum:** Here you'll see what it was like to live in a prairie dwelling made out of chunks of grassy soil. You'll also see an enormous plow and barbed-wire sculptures of a bison and a Native American on horseback.

North Platte

★ **Buffalo Bill Ranch State Historical Park:** This is where Buffalo Bill Cody practiced his Wild West Show and held the country's first rodeo. Today, you can tour the ranch.

★ **Nebraskaland Days:** North Platte taps into its Wild West heritage with this June festival. It features the Buffalo Bill Rodeo, a Mexican fiesta, a kids' parade, and much more.

Buffalo Bill Ranch State Historical Park

SAND HILLS REGION

THINGS TO DO: Hike through the wilderness, see awesome waterfalls, enjoy some Danish pancakes, explore underground caverns, or stay overnight in a tepee!

Dannebrog

★ **Grundlovsfest:** If you're here in early June, don't miss this Danish festival. You'll enjoy *aebleskiver* (Danish pancakes), a duck race, Danish dancers, and much more. Dannebrog is called the Danish Capital of Nebraska because so many immigrants from Denmark settled in the area.

★ **National Liars' Hall of Fame:** Located in the Lille Mermaid Gift Shop, this museum is full of gadgets that are supposed to do amazing things—but don't. Thus, it's a tribute to the art of lying. No kidding!

Scotia

★ **Happy Jack Chalk Mine:** For an underground adventure, check out this maze of mining tunnels. It has more than 6,000 feet (1,830 m) of caverns.

Stuart

★ **Beaver Creek Canyon:** At this site you can take part in a variety of Native American learning programs. You can learn Native skills and crafts, experience a day in Indian life, and even stay overnight in a tepee. These events are First Nebraskans Living History Programs, sponsored by Spirit in the Wind. Be sure to make reservations in advance.

Halsey

★ **Nebraska National Forest (Bessey Ranger District):** Climb up the rangers' lookout tower in Halsey for an awesome view of the forest. Just imagine what it took to plant all those trees by hand! Volunteers planted them in the early 1900s. The forest is a great place for camping, hiking, and picnicking.

Long Pine

★ **Long Pine State Recreation Area:** This is a great area for outdoor adventures. You can hike through acres of wilderness, fish for trout in Pine Creek, gaze down on scenic canyons, and see all kinds of wildlife.

Valentine

★ **Fort Niobrara National Wildlife Refuge:** After a wildlife-watching hike, start here for a fantastic canoe trip on the Niobrara River. You'll pass several waterfalls, including Smith Falls. Cascading down 75 feet (23 m), it's Nebraska's highest waterfall.

THE PANHANDLE

THINGS TO DO: Follow ancient fossil footprints, climb rocky landmarks the pioneers knew, see where early hunters killed hundreds of bison, see cars sticking up out of the ground, or take a covered-wagon trip, complete with cookout!

Bridgeport

★ **Courthouse and Jail Rocks:** These unusual rock formations were important landmarks for pioneers as they followed the North Platte River along the Oregon Trail.

★ **Pioneer Trails Museum:** Here you'll learn all about the westbound pioneers and how they lived.

Carhenge

Alliance

★ **Carhenge:** This wacky monument is modeled after England's Stonehenge, where huge stones stand in a circle. But at Carhenge, old cars are sticking up out of the ground instead!

Bayard

★ **Chimney Rock National Historic Site:** "Towering to the heavens"— that's how one pioneer described this rocky landmark. Gaze up at the tall, pointy spire, and you'll see why it was one of the best-known markers along the Oregon Trail.

★ **Oregon Trail Wagon Train:** Join this tour, and you'll head out for a real covered-wagon trek and an old-time cookout in the shadow of Chimney Rock.

Gering

★ **Scotts Bluff National Monument:** This majestic rock formation was a landmark for Native Americans, fur trappers, and pioneers. On summer weekends, you can take part in living history programs to relive the Oregon Trail experience.

Scotts Bluff National Monument

★ **Oregon Trail Museum and Visitor Center:** Watch an audio-visual presentation and explore exhibits on the pioneers and the area's geology. The museum is on the grounds of Scotts Bluff National Monument.

Crawford

★ **Hudson-Meng Bison Kill Research & Visitor Center:** Early hunters lived here 10,000 years ago and killed hundreds of bison for food. Learn about their lives at the site's museum, and then tour the surrounding bone beds.

★ **Intertribal Powwow:** In June, drummers, dancers, and singers from several states come to Fort Robinson State Park to celebrate their traditional culture. This is the largest competitive powwow in western Nebraska.

Crawford area

★ **Agate Fossil Beds National Monument:** Wander the trails on this site, and you'll discover an amazing array of ancient fossils. You'll also see ancient sand dunes and the petrified spiral burrows of prehistoric land beavers.

★ **Toadstool Park:** You're now in Nebraska's Badlands. Among the park's weird, windswept rock formations, you'll see some fascinating fossil footprints. Thirty million years ago, rhino relatives and piglike creatures left their tracks in the wet sand.

Chadron

★ **Museum of the Fur Trade:** At this museum, you'll explore the world of trappers and traders of many nationalities and the Native Americans with whom they worked.

Harrison/Chadron/Gordon

★ **Pine Ridge region:** Here you'll see some of Nebraska's most beautiful scenery—deep forests, towering ridges, rugged cliffs, rippling streams, and abundant wildlife. Trails for hiking or horseback riding wind through the wilderness.

WRITING PROJECTS

Check out these ideas for creating a campaign brochure and writing you-are-there narratives. Or research the migration paths of settlers and explorers.

ART PROJECTS

You can illustrate the state song, or create a great PowerPoint presentation, or learn about the state quarter and design your own.

TIMELINE

What happened when? This timeline highlights important events in the state's history—and shows what was happening throughout the United States at the same time.

FAST FACTS

Use this section to find fascinating facts about state symbols, land area and population statistics, weather, sports teams, and much more.

GLOSSARY

Remember the Words to Know from the chapters in this book? They're all collected here.

SCIENCE, TECHNOLOGY, ENGINEERING, & MATH PROJECTS

Make weather maps, graph population statistics, and research endangered species that live in the state.

120

PRIMARY VS. SECONDARY SOURCES

121

So what are primary and secondary sources and what's the diff? This section explains all that and where you can find them.

BIOGRAPHICAL DICTIONARY

133

This at-a-glance guide highlights some of the state's most important and influential people. Visit this section and read up about their contributions to the state, the country, and the world.

RESOURCES

Books and much more. Take a look at these additional sources for information about the state.

138

WRITING PROJECTS

Create an Election Brochure or Web Site!

Run for office!

Throughout this book, you've read about some of the issues that concern Nebraska today.

★ As a candidate for governor of Nebraska, create a campaign brochure or Web site.

★ Explain how you meet the qualifications to be governor of Nebraska, and talk about the three or four major issues you'll focus on if you're elected.

★ Remember, you'll be responsible for Nebraska's budget. How would you spend the taxpayers' money?

SEE: Chapter Seven, pages 85–93.

Compare and Contrast— When, Why, and How Did They Come?

Compare the migration and explorations of Nebraska's Native people and its first European explorers. Tell about:

★ When their migrations began

★ How they traveled

★ Why they migrated

★ Where their journeys began and ended

★ What they found when they arrived

SEE: Chapters Two and Three, pages 25–37 and 39–43.

Write a Memoir, Journal, or Editorial for Your School Newspaper!

Picture Yourself . . .

★ On a vision quest. In solitude, you wait for visions to come that might reveal the animal whose spirit will give you strength, guidance, and protection. Describe the experience and imagine what animal's spirit might guide you.

SEE: Chapter Two, page 36.

★ As an Exoduster settling in Nebraska. Would you be excited by the move to the West? What challenges would you face?

SEE: Chapter Three, pages 56–57.

★ As a Nebraskan during World War II. Would you be working in a factory making supplies? Or would you be harvesting crops used to feed soldiers?

SEE: Chapter Five, pages 63–64.

Weapons factory

ART PROJECTS

Create a PowerPoint Presentation or Visitors' Guide
Welcome to Nebraska!

Nebraska is a great place to visit and to live! From its natural beauty to its bustling cities and historic sites, there's plenty to see and do. In your PowerPoint presentation or brochure, highlight 10 to 15 of Nebraska's amazing landmarks. Be sure to include:

★ a map of the state showing where these sites are located

★ photos, illustrations, Web links, natural history facts, geographic stats, climate and weather info, and descriptions of plant and wildlife

SEE: Chapters One and Nine, pages 9–23 and 105–115.

Illustrate the Lyrics to the Nebraska State Song
("Beautiful Nebraska")

Use markers, paints, photos, collage, colored pencils, or computer graphics to illustrate the lyrics to "Beautiful Nebraska," the state song. Turn your illustrations into a picture book, or scan them into a PowerPoint and add music.

SEE: The lyrics to "Beautiful Nebraska" on page 128.

State Quarter Project

From 1999 to 2008, the U.S. Mint introduced new quarters commemorating each of the 50 states in the order that they were admitted into the Union. Each state's quarter features a unique design on its reverse, or back.

GO TO: www.factsfornow.scholastic.com. Enter the keyword **Nebraska** and look for the link to the Nebraska quarter.

★ Research and write an essay explaining the significance of each image, who designed the quarter, and who chose the final design.

★ Design your own Nebraska quarter. What images would you choose for the reverse?

★ Make a poster showing the Nebraska quarter and label each image.

SCIENCE, TECHNOLOGY, ENGINEERING, & MATH PROJECTS

Graph Population Statistics!

★ Compare population statistics (such as ethnic background, birth, death, and literacy rates) in Nebraska counties or major cities.

★ In your graph or chart, look at population density, and write sentences describing what the population statistics show; graph one set of population statistics, and write a paragraph explaining what the graphs reveal.
SEE: Chapter Six, pages 70–73.

Create a Weather Map of Nebraska!

Use your knowledge of Nebraska's geography to research and identify conditions that result in specific weather events. What is it about the geography of Nebraska that makes it vulnerable to things such as tornadoes, hailstorms, and blizzards? Create a weather map or poster that shows the weather patterns over the state. Include a caption explaining the technology used to measure weather phenomena.
SEE: Chapter One, pages 17–19.

Track Endangered Species

Using your knowledge of Nebraska's wildlife, research what animals and plants are endangered or threatened. Find out what the state is doing to protect these species. Chart known populations of the animals and plants, and report on changes in certain geographical areas.
SEE: Chapter One, page 20.

A black-footed ferret

PRIMARY VS. SECONDARY SOURCES

What's the Diff?

Your teacher may require at least one or two primary sources and one or two secondary sources for your assignment. So, what's the difference between the two?

★ **Primary sources are original.** You are reading the actual words of someone's diary, journal, letter, autobiography, or interview. Primary sources can also be photographs, maps, prints, cartoons, news/film footage, posters, first-person newspaper articles, drawings, musical scores, and recordings. By the way, when you conduct a survey, interview someone, shoot a video, or take photographs to include in a project—you are creating primary sources!

★ **Secondary sources are what you find in encyclopedias, textbooks, articles, biographies, and almanacs.** These are written by a person or group of people who tell about something that happened to someone else. Secondary sources also recount what another person said or did. This book is an example of a secondary source.

Now that you know what primary sources are—where can you find them?

★ **Your school or local library:** Check the library catalog for collections of original writings, government documents, musical scores, and so on. Some of this material may be stored on microfilm.

★ **Historical societies:** These organizations keep historical documents, photographs, and other materials. Staff members can help you find what you are looking for. History museums are also great places to see primary sources firsthand.

★ **The Internet:** There are lots of sites that have primary sources you can download and use in a project or assignment.

TIMELINE

★ ★ ★

U.S. Events	**1600**	Nebraska Events

c. 1650
Native Americans first acquire
horses from Spaniards.

1682
René-Robert Cavelier, Sieur de La Salle,
claims more than 1 million square miles (2.6
million sq km) of territory in the Mississippi
River basin for France, naming it Louisiana.

1700

1700
Nebraska is home to Pawnees, Omahas,
Poncas, Otos, Sioux, and many other peoples.

1714
Frenchman Étienne de Véniard,
Sieur de Bourgmont, is the first
European to reach Nebraska.

1720
Pawnees and Otos defeat Spanish troops
near the fork of the Loup and Platte rivers.

Spanish troops fighting Pawnees and Otos

1739
French fur traders Pierre and Paul
Mallet cross Nebraska.

1763
The French and Indian War ends; Nebraska
passes from French to Spanish rule.

1776
Thirteen American colonies declare their
independence from Great Britain.

1800

1803
In the Louisiana Purchase, Nebraska
comes under U.S. control.

1804
Meriwether Lewis and William Clark
explore eastern Nebraska and meet with
Native Americans at Council Bluff.

1812–15
The United States and Great Britain
fight the War of 1812.

1819
Fort Atkinson is established
near today's Fort Lisa.

U.S. Events

Nebraska Events

1820
Major Stephen Long explores the Great Plains, including Nebraska; he calls the region the Great American Desert.

1823
Bellevue becomes Nebraska's first permanent white settlement.

1830
The Indian Removal Act forces eastern Native American groups to relocate west of the Mississippi River.

1843
Pioneers begin taking the Oregon Trail across Nebraska.

1846–48
The United States fights a war with Mexico over western territories in the Mexican War.

1848
Fort Kearny is established to protect westbound travelers.

1851
In the Fort Laramie Treaty, several Native American groups agree to let white settlers cross Indian lands along the Platte River.

1854
Congress passes the Kansas-Nebraska Act, establishing Nebraska Territory.

1861–65
The American Civil War is fought between the Northern Union and the Southern Confederacy; it ends with the surrender of the Confederate army, led by General Robert E. Lee.

1862
The Homestead Act offers free land to settlers in Nebraska.

1865
Construction of the transcontinental railroad across Nebraska begins.

1866
The U.S. Congress approves the Fourteenth Amendment to the U.S. Constitution, granting citizenship to African Americans.

1867
Nebraska becomes the 37th U.S. state.

1870s
Swarms of grasshoppers destroy Nebraska's crops.

U.S. Events

Nebraska Events

1879
African American settlers called Exodusters begin moving into Nebraska.

1880s
Omaha is a national center for the meatpacking industry.

1900

1915
The Lincoln Highway is completed through Nebraska.

1917-18
The United States engages in World War I.

1929
The stock market crashes, plunging the United States more deeply into the Great Depression.

1930s
Nebraskans plant millions of trees as shelterbelts for soil conservation.

1937
Nebraska's unicameral legislature meets for the first time.

1941-45
The United States engages in World War II.

1960
Nebraska's urban population outnumbers its rural residents.

1964-73
The United States engages in the Vietnam War.

1982
Initiative 300 bars large corporations from buying Nebraska farmland.

1987
New tax laws are passed to benefit businesses and keep them in the state.

2000

2001
Terrorists hijack four U.S. aircraft and crash them into the World Trade Center in New York City, the Pentagon in Arlington, Virginia, and a Pennsylvania field, killing thousands.

2003
The United States and coalition forces invade Iraq.

2005
Nebraska governor Mike Johanns is appointed U.S. secretary of agriculture.

2012
Nebraska experiences the driest summer in state history.

GLOSSARY

★ ★ ★

aquifer an underground layer of soil or loose rock that holds water

archaeologists people who study the remains of past human societies

ballot a sheet of paper on which people mark their voting choices. (Some places conduct voting with electronic machines rather than by paper ballots.)

buttes narrow, flat-topped hills with very steep sides

deity a being regarded as a god

drought a period of little or no rainfall

equinox one of the two days of the year when day and night are of equal length

extinct no longer existing

fossil the remains or prints of ancient animals or plants left in stone

game animals hunted for food

legislature the lawmaking body of a state, country, or other political unit

migrating traveling to another location, usually covering a long distance

sod soil thickly packed together with grass and roots

transcontinental crossing an entire continent

FAST FACTS

★ ★ ★

State Symbols

Statehood date	March 1, 1867, the 37th state
Origin of state name	From the Oto Indian word meaning "flat water" describing the Platte River
State capital	Lincoln
State nickname	Cornhusker State, Tree Planters' State
State motto	"Equality before the law"
State bird	Western meadowlark
State flower	Goldenrod
State insect	Honeybee
State gem	Blue chalcedony
State rock	Prairie agate
State fossil	Mammoth
State song	"Beautiful Nebraska" (see lyrics on page 128)
State tree	Cottonwood
State grass	Little bluestem
State mammal	Whitetail deer
State fair	Lincoln (late August–early September)

State seal

Geography

Total area; rank	77,354 square miles (200,347 sq km); 16th
Land; rank	76,872 square miles (199,098 sq km); 15th
Water; rank	481 square miles (1,246 sq km); 42nd
Inland water; rank	481 square miles (1,246 sq km); 34th
Geographic center	Custer County, 10 miles (16 km) northwest of Broken Bow
Latitude	40° N to 43° N
Longitude	95° 25' W to 104° W
Highest point	Panorama Point, 5,424 feet (1,653 m), located in Kimball County
Lowest point	Missouri River at 840 feet (256 m), in Richardson County
Largest city	Omaha
Number of counties	93
Longest river	Missouri River, 385 miles (620 km)

Population

Population; rank (2010 census):	1,826,341; 38th
Density (2010 census):	24 persons per square mile (9 per sq km)
Population distribution (2010 census):	73% urban, 27% rural
Race (2010 census):	White persons: 82.1%

Black persons: 4.4%

Asian persons: 1.7%

American Indian and Alaska Native persons: 0.8%

Native Hawaiian and Other
   Pacific Islander persons: 0.1%

Persons reporting two or more races: 1.6%

Hispanic or Latino persons: 9.2%

People of some other race: 0.1%

Weather

Record high temperature	118°F (48°C) at Minden on July 24, 1936; at Hartington on July 17, 1936; and at Geneva on July 15, 1934
Record low temperature	−47°F (−44°C) at Bridgeport, on February 12, 1899; and at Oshkosh on December 22,1989
Average July temperature	76°F (24°C)
Average January temperature	23°F (−5°C)
Average yearly precipitation	23 inches (58 cm)

State flag

STATE SONG

★ ★ ★

"Beautiful Nebraska"

Music by Jim Fras; Words by Jim Fras and Guy G. Miller

Nebraska legislators discussed the selection of a state song through several sessions. They finally selected "Beautiful Nebraska," which was composed by Jim Fras of Lincoln. Fras, a Russian refugee who came to Lincoln in 1952, is a professional entertainer and composer. The song became the state's official song on June 21, 1967.

Beautiful Nebraska, peaceful prairieland,
Laced with many rivers and the hills of sand;
Dark green valleys cradled in the earth,
Rain and sunshine bring abundant birth.

Beautiful Nebraska, as you look around,
You will find a rainbow reaching to the ground;
All these wonders by the Master's hand,
Beautiful Nebraska land.

We are so proud of this state where we live.
There is no place that has so much to give.

Beautiful Nebraska, as you look around,
You will find a rainbow reaching to the ground;
All these wonders by the Master's hand,
Beautiful Nebraska land.

NATU AL AREAS AN--
HISTORIC SITES

★ ★ ★

National Monument

Nebraska is home to three national monuments. They are the *Agate Fossil Beds National Monument*, which is renowned for its mammal fossils from the Miocene epoch; the *Homestead National Monument of America*, which is the site of one of the first homestead claims under the Homestead Act of 1862; and *Scotts Bluff National Monument,* which marks a promontory on the Oregon Trail.

National Recreational Rivers

The *Missouri National Recreational River* protects two stretches of the Missouri River in Nebraska. It also stands as a site for the Lewis and Clark expedition.

National Scenic River

The *Niobrara National Scenic River* flows past six different ecosystems, diverse wildlife, and local and historical architecture.

National Historic Sites

Nebraska's sole national historic site is the *Chimney Rock National Historic Site,* found on the pathway of the Oregon Trail. It was an inspiring landmark for the pioneers.

National Historic Trail

Nebraska has four national historic trails that cross through its borders, each with its own historical significance: including the *California National Historic Trail*, the *Lewis and Clark National Historic Trail*, the *Oregon Trail National Historic Trail*, and the *Pony Express National Historic Trail.*

National Forests

Nebraska has two national forests: the *McKelvie National Forest* in Cherry County, and the *Nebraska National Forest in Blaine*, Dawes, Sioux, and Thomas counties, which stands as the largest hand-planted forest in the United States.

State Parks and Forests

Nebraska has 84 state parks and recreation areas, including *Fort Kearny State Recreation Area,* which is home to the fort that protected travelers heading west on the Oregon Trail; *Arbor Lodge State Historical Park,* which is J. Sterling Morton's elegant mansion; and *Buffalo Bill Ranch State Recreation Park,* which was William Frederick Cody's home for more than 30 years.

SPORTS TEAMS

★ ★ ★

NCAA Teams (Division I)

Creighton University *Bluejays*
University of Nebraska *Cornhuskers*

University of Nebraska Cornhuskers

CULTURAL INSTITUTIONS

★ ★ ★

Libraries

The *Nebraska State Library* (Lincoln) is the oldest library in the state and is primarily a law library.

The *University of Nebraska at Lincoln* has the state's largest library collection.

Museums

The *Joslyn Art Museum* (Omaha) has a noted collection of western art, as well as collections ranging from ancient works to modern art.

The *Museum of the Fur Trade* (Chadron) has a large collection of Indian artifacts, early guns, and other fur trade relics.

The *Sheldon Memorial Art Gallery at the University of Nebraska* (Lincoln) houses modern American paintings and sculpture.

Stuhr Museum of the Prairie Pioneer (Grand Island) features the restored Railroad Town, reminiscent of the 1890s. A bank, general store, and post office are among 60 frontier buildings there.

The *University of Nebraska State Museum* (Lincoln) has one of the world's largest mammoth fossil collections.

Performing Arts

Opera Omaha (Omaha) performs classic operas from around the world.

The *Lincoln Symphony Orchestra* (Lincoln) presents a blend of music, theater, and performances for culture lovers of all ages.

Universities and Colleges

In 2012, Nebraska had 7 public and 21 private institutions of higher learning.

ANNUAL EVENTS

January–March

St. Patrick's Day Celebration in O'Neill (March)

Sandhill Crane Migration in Grand Island, Hastings, and Kearney (March–April)

April–June

Arbor Day statewide (April)

Grundlovsfest, or Danish Day, in Dannebrog (June)

NCAA College World Series in Omaha (June)

Nebraskaland Days in North Platte (June)

Swedish Festivals in Oakland and Stromsburg (June)

Willa Cather Spring Conference in Red Cloud (June)

North Platte Nightly Rodeo (June–July)

July–September

Fur Trade Days in Chadron (July)

John C. Fremont Days in Fremont (July)

Old Mill Days in Neligh (July)

Oregon Trail Days in Gering (July)

State Fourth of July Celebration in Seward (July)

Wayne Chicken Show in Wayne (July)

Winnebago Powwow in Winnebago (July)

Czech Festival in Wilber (August)

Nebraska's Big Rodeo in Burwell (August)

Nebraska State Fair in Grand Island (late August–early September)

Husker Harvest Days in Grand Island (September)

River City Rodeo and Stock Show in Omaha (September)

October–December

Cowboy Poetry Gathering in Valentine (October)

Oktoberfest in Sidney (October)

Danish Christmas Festival in Dannebrog (December)

BIOGRAPHICAL DICTIONARY

Grace Abbott (1873–1939) was a reformer who fought to protect children's rights. She was especially concerned about children who had to work long hours in factories for low wages. In 1917, she became the head of the Children's Bureau of the U.S. Department of Labor. She was born in Grand Island.

Bess Streeter Aldrich (1881–1954) was the author of more than 100 short stories, many magazine articles, and novels, including children's books. Born in Iowa, she later lived in Elmwood.

Grover Cleveland "Pete" Alexander (1887–1950) was a baseball pitcher for the Philadelphia Phillies, the Chicago Cubs, and the St. Louis Cardinals. He pitched 373 winning games during his major league baseball career. He was born in Elba.

Grover Cleveland "Pete" Alexander

Fred Astaire

Clayton Anderson (1959–) is a former NASA astronaut who was chosen to live and work on the International Space Station in 2007. He spent 152 days on the station and often passed the time by playing trivia games with mission control members on the ground in Houston, Texas. Anderson was born in Omaha.

Fred Astaire (1899–1987) was an actor famous for his smooth ballroom dancing. In many of his movies, his dance partner was Ginger Rogers. He was born in Omaha.

Bil Baird (1904–1987) was a puppeteer whose career peaked with his puppet Charlemagne, a raggedy-looking lion that appeared on TV in the 1950s. He was born in Grand Island.

Marlon Brando (1924–2004) was a movie actor who won Academy Awards for his roles in *On the Waterfront* and *The Godfather*. He was born in Omaha.

Mildred Brown See page 66.

William Jennings Bryan See page 89.

Warren Buffett See page 98.

134

Johnny Carson

Johnny Carson (1925–2005) was an entertainer who hosted *The Tonight Show*, a nighttime TV talk show, from 1962 to 1992. Born in Iowa, Carson grew up in Norfolk.

Willa Cather See page 76.

Dick Cavett (1936–) is a TV talk show host known for his easygoing style and his focus on important issues. Born in Gibbon, he began his career as a comedy writer for Johnny Carson's *The Tonight Show*. These days, he writes columns for the online *New York Times*.

Dick Cheney (1941–) was born in Lincoln and moved to Wyoming as a child. He was a U.S. congressman from Wyoming, U.S. secretary of defense, and vice president of the United States.

William Frederick "Buffalo Bill" Cody (1846–1917) was a showman who was best known for Buffalo Bill's Wild West Show, which he opened in Omaha in 1883. Scouts Rest Ranch was his home in North Platte.

Crazy Horse (1840–1877) was a leader of the Oglala Lakota people during their battles against the U.S. government. In 1876, he led his warriors to victory over General George Custer at the Battle of Little Bighorn in present-day Montana.

Angel DeCora (1871–1919) was an artist known for her Native American themes. She was born on the Winnebago Reservation in Dakota County.

Aaron Douglas See page 80.

Harold Edgerton (1903–1990) invented the strobe light in 1931. This super-fast blinking light made it possible to take stop-motion photos. The Edgerton Explorit Center, a hands-on science center, is in Aurora. Edgerton was born in Fremont.

Rosalie LaFlesche Farley (1861–1900) was the daughter of Omaha chief Joseph LaFlesche. She helped Omahas understand their rights and fight legal battles. She also acted as a go-between for Omahas and U.S. government agents.

Edward Flanagan (1886–1948) was a Catholic priest who founded Boys Town in Omaha in 1917. This organization for homeless and troubled young people is now called Girls and Boys Town.

William "Buffalo Bill" Cody

Henry Fonda (1905–1982) was an actor who appeared in *Young Mr. Lincoln, The Grapes of Wrath,* and dozens of other films. He was born in Grand Island.

Daniel Freeman See page 51.

Joyce C. Hall (1891–1982) was the founder of Hallmark Cards. When he was 16, he and his two brothers started a postcard company. It grew to become one of the world's most successful greeting card companies. He was born in David City.

Howard Hanson (1896–1981) was a composer and conductor. In 1944, he received the Pulitzer Prize for music. He was born in Wahoo.

Wilma Pitchford Hays (1907–2006) was a children's book author who was born in Fullerton.

Marg Helgenberger (1958–) is an actress best known for playing Catherine Willows on *CSI: Crime Scene Investigation.* Her movie credits include *In Good Company* and *Mr. Brooks.* She was born in North Bend.

Marg Helgenberger

Malcolm X

Ben Kuroki See page 63.

Swoosie Kurtz (1944–) is an actress. She has appeared in Broadway plays, movies, and TV shows and received many best-actress nominations and awards. She was born in Omaha.

John L. Loos (1918–2011) was a historian known for his writings on the Lewis and Clark Expedition, which explored the territories of the Louisiana Purchase. He served as professor at Louisiana State University, specializing in the history of the American West.

Malcolm X See page 65.

Max Mathews (1926–2011) was a computer engineer who developed the first programs that allowed the user to choose what tones to hear on a computer. His work laid the groundwork for the sounds now made by synthesizers, drum machines, and laptop computers.

Gerardo Meza See page 78.

Patsy Takemoto Mink See page 92.

J. Sterling Morton See page 21.

José Lopez Naranjo See page 41.

Red Cloud

John G. Neihardt (1881–1973) wrote *A Cycle of the West* and *Black Elk Speaks*. He was named poet laureate of Nebraska in 1921. Born in Illinois, he later lived in Bancroft.

Nick Nolte (1941–) is a movie and TV actor. He is known for his action movies, such as *48 Hours,* as well as for serious dramas and independent films. He was born in Omaha.

Tillie Olsen (1912–2007) was a writer and an activist who spoke out for the rights of women, immigrants, and poor workers. Her novel *Yonnondio* is her best-known work. She was born in Omaha.

Kay A. Orr (1939–) was the first Republican woman to be elected governor in the United States, and to date, the only woman to have served as governor of Nebraska. She previously served as Nebraska state treasurer.

Edwin Perkins (1889–1961) invented Kool-Aid in 1927. Born in Iowa, he moved to Nebraska with his family when he was four.

John J. Pershing (1860–1948) commanded the American Expeditionary Forces in Europe during World War I. Born in Missouri, he kept a home in Lincoln.

Susan LaFlesche Picotte See page 56.

Red Cloud (1822–1909) was an Oglala Sioux leader who was born near present-day North Platte. His resistance to settlers led to the Fort Laramie Treaty of 1868. The town of Red Cloud is named for him.

Andy Roddick (1982–) is a tennis player who won the U.S. Open in 2003. He holds the world record for the fastest serve, at 153 miles (246 km) per hour. He was born in Omaha.

Mari Sandoz (1896–1966) was a novelist who wrote about the hardships of Nebraska homesteaders, immigrants, women settlers, and Native Americans. She was born in Mirage Flats.

Andy Roddick

Reuben Snake

Reuben Snake See page 72.

Ted Sorensen (1928–2010) was an adviser and speechwriter for U.S. president John F. Kennedy from 1961 to 1964. He was later a best-selling author, writing mainly about American politics. He was born in Lincoln.

Standing Bear (1834?–1908) was a Ponca chief who led his people from Oklahoma back to Nebraska. Standing Bear was detained by the U.S. Army and filed suit to be allowed to return home. In the course of the suit, the judge declared that "an Indian is a person within the meaning of the law and the Poncas must be set free." This was the first time Native Americans were declared legal persons.

Hilary Swank (1974–) is an actor who appeared in *Buffy the Vampire Slayer* and *The Next Karate Kid.* She won Academy Awards for her roles in *Boys Don't Cry* and *Million Dollar Baby.* She was born in Lincoln.

Gabrielle Union (1972–) is an actress who appeared in the movies *Bring It On, Deliver Us from Eva, Bad Boys II,* and *Breakin' All the Rules.* She was born in Omaha.

Étienne de Véniard, Sieur de Bourgmont See page 40.

Daniel Lawrence Whitney (1963–) was born in Pawnee City and is a comedian known as Larry the Cable Guy.

Evan Williams (1972–), born in Clarks, founded several Internet companies, including two of the most popular: Blogger and Twitter.

Paula Zahn (1956–) is a TV newscaster. From 2003 to 2007, she hosted *Paula Zahn Now* on CNN. She was born in Omaha.

Darryl F. Zanuck (1902–1979) was a film producer and director. He produced films such as *How Green Was My Valley, The Grapes of Wrath,* and *Twelve O'clock High.* He was born in Wahoo.

Gabrielle Union

RESOURCES

★ ★ ★

BOOKS

Nonfiction

Bjorklund, Ruth, and Marlee Richards. *Nebraska*. New York: Marshall Cavendish Benchmark, 2010.

Burrows, John. *Lewis and Clark: Blazing a Trail West*. New York: Sterling, 2008.

Keating, Frank. *The Trial of Standing Bear*. Oklahoma City, Okla.: Oklahoma Heritage Association, 2008.

McNeese, Tim. *The Louisiana Purchase: Growth of a Nation*. New York: Chelsea House, 2009.

Reis, Ronald A. *Buffalo Bill Cody*. New York: Chelsea House, 2010.

Santella, Andrew. *The French and Indian War*. New York: Children's Press, 2012.

Fiction

Aldrich, Bess Streeter. *A Lantern in Her Hand*. New York: Puffin Books, 1997.

Brown, Marion Marsh. *Stuart's Landing: A Story of Pioneer Nebraska*. Philadelphia: Westminster Press, 1960.

Cather, Willa. *O Pioneers!* (Many editions available).

Figley, Marty Rhodes, and Shelly O. Hass (illustrator). *The Schoolchildren's Blizzard*. Minneapolis: Carolrhoda, 2004.

Gray, Dianne. *Holding Up the Earth*. Boston: Houghton Mifflin, 2000.

Kooser, Ted. *The Blizzard Voices*. Lincoln: University of Nebraska Press, 2006.

Thomas, Dorothy. *The Getaway and Other Stories*. Lincoln: University of Nebraska Press, 2002.

INDEX

★ ★ ★

AUTHOR'S TIPS AND SOURCE NOTES

★   ★   ★

In researching this book, I especially enjoyed reading about west-bound pioneers on the Oregon Trail. It's incredible how people managed to survive their journey. The Nebraska State Historical Society has a terrific Web site that provides a great overview of early Nebraska history, starting with prehistoric times. Other useful sources were *History of Nebraska,* by James C. Olson and Ronald C. Naugle, and *Nebraska: An Illustrated History,* by Frederick C. Luebke.